T0321068

PRAISE FOR *REINVENT*

"With exponentially advancing technologies and COVID-type viruses, companies are going to have to adapt or perish. Faisal Hoque's book *REINVENT* brilliantly illustrates how businesses can change their mindsets, attitudes, and assumptions about how they operate and thrive in the midst of change; it is an approachable guide to the art of business reinvention. Faisal explains complex concepts in a way that most people will be able to understand."

—**VIVEK WADHWA,** award-winning academic; entrepreneur; former Distinguished Fellow at Harvard Law School, Carnegie Mellon School of Engineering, and Emory University and author of five best-selling books, including *From Incremental to Exponential*

"In my world, you either 'learn to ski or get swept away by the avalanche.' The avalanche in business is change—massive and coming faster and faster. As Faisal Hoque points out in *REINVENT*, the answer is more than adopting new digital tools—it requires changing the entire mindset of the organization to use those tools and learn how to deal with the ever-changing world."

—**HAP KLOPP,** author and founder of The North Face

"A digital transformation ideally changes everything about how a company works. But it often fails to achieve this end, wasting considerable sums in the process. Faisal Hoque's invaluable book *REINVENT* shows how such holistic change is especially necessary since the pandemic completely upended corporate America's assumptions about its customers and employees.

He tells us how to prepare for and then conduct a successful transformation, reminding us of the extreme importance of obtaining buy-in by everyone impacted—before embarking on the journey. CIOs like myself know that continuous change is exhausting, expensive, and difficult, and organizations can easily get sidelined into the technicalities of tool- and package-fitting.

But Hoque also warns us against viewing technology as a savior able to correct everything wrong with an organization.

This is a book I will consult again and again."

—**ATTI RIAZI,** senior vice president and CIO, Hearst, and former assistant secretary general and chief information technology officer, United Nations

"If you are a leader driving business transformation, *REINVENT* is a must-read! Leaders who assume they understand the ramifications of technological change often focus on a select few silo issues. With *REINVENT*, Faisal Hoque points out that there's so much more involved—from leadership itself to the value of understanding what the workforce of tomorrow is going to demand in the workplace. Read this book today!"

—**DANIEL BURRUS,** *New York Times* best-selling author of
Flash Foresight and *The Anticipatory Organization*

"*REINVENT* is important and relevant reading for both established and new business leaders. Faisal Hoque shows how organizations can realize the promise inherent in new technologies without making the same mistakes that have dogged large transformation efforts in the past. The importance of this book lies in the author's ability to show readers how technology-driven change requires new mindsets and new approaches. It lays out a road map for how to succeed in the realm of digital transformations."

—**ANANDHI BHARADWAJ,** vice dean for faculty and research, Goizueta
Endowed Chair in E-Commerce, and professor of information
systems and operations management, Emory University

"Digital natives are often disruptors, but when it comes to traditional firms, the issue is more complex. We called it digital reinvention in our 2017 article in *Sloan Management Review*. Faisal Hoque not only chooses the term for his new book title, but he also eloquently helps debug one core myth about tech. That is that tech replaces everything, from replacing intermediaries by platforms and automating workers' tasks to recommending what you watch on TikTok. What tech does not replace is management leadership to help augment an organization with technology in a way that companies become stronger (reinvented) with technologies. The author also provides a solid framework (LIFTS) that leaders would be wise to follow to thrive in the future."

—**JACQUES BUGHIN,** CEO, Machaon Advisory; former senior partner,
McKinsey and Company; senior advisor, United Nations, Antler,
and Fortino Capital; and professor, Solvay Business School

"Reinvention is a decidedly challenging undertaking. Faisal Hoque's *REINVENT* offers an easy-to-follow, comprehensive playbook so that companies and organizations can avoid the reinvention pitfalls that so many experience. Read this timely book—let it guide you and your chances of success are significantly strengthened."

–**SUBIR CHOWDHURY**, chairman and CEO, ASI Consulting Group, LLC; best-selling author of *The Difference*; and named one of the 50 most influential management thinkers in the world by Thinkers50

"We as people and businesses have done nothing but transform for centuries. And in my lifetime, we have added the ability to form, create, and mold the digital aspects of our lives, our customers' lives, what we build, create, maintain, and service. So where do we go the next ten, twenty, fifty years, and beyond? In centuries to come, how will people look back at our time and what was accomplished and missed?

In this amazing book, we see the opportunities and the obligation we have to replicate past successes and do better. Enjoy!"

–**MARNE MARTIN**, chief strategy officer and global president, IFS, and one of the Top 50 Women Leaders in Saas of 2022

"*REINVENT* is a timely playbook for leaders serious about positioning their organizations to successfully compete in the turbulent post-COVID economy. This latest book from Faisal Hoque is a valuable resource filled with powerful examples, deep insights, and practical advice. Leaders who can reinvent their organizations will not only succeed but will also thrive in these challenging times. Reinvention is not a destination; it's a journey.

Organizations must reinvent by incorporating the digital mindset, embracing highly collaborative leadership style, and creating an innovative culture with an empowered workforce. *REINVENT* is mandatory reading for those navigating this challenging, essential, and rewarding journey."

–**SHAMIM MOHAMMAD**, executive vice president and chief information and technology officer, CarMax, and independent member of board of directors, UNFI

"It is no secret that most new products fail. Reinvention is key for long-term success, but efforts to reinvent fail even more. With his latest book, Faisal Hoque makes a convincing case for trying anyway, and, more importantly, offers the blueprint, examples, and best practices to succeed. A highly recommended read for your transformation journey!"

—CAN (JOHN) USLAY, PHD, vice dean of innovation and strategic partnerships and professor of marketing, Rutgers Business School

"Many books on digital transformation already feel dated. After all, most organizations have already made a big digitization push and have realized that their need for reinvention is ongoing. What Faisal Hoque has done with *REINVENT* is to acknowledge that transformation is more than digital or data; it is a wholesale cultural reinvention of the organization and its mission, along with its inner and outer relationships. What's more, it is ongoing and iterative. Faisal's expert guidance throughout the book is like having a trusted advisor at your side the whole way."

—KATE O'NEILL, author of *A Future So Bright* and *Tech Humanist*; founder and chief tech humanist, KO Insights; and 2020 Thinkers50 Radar

"Technology is more than a fad or a requirement of businesses. In *REINVENT*, Faisal Hoque highlights the fact that mastering technology is essential to mastering business, period, and is directly related to business performance. It's no longer possible to simply get by; thriving with technology is essential to thriving in business today. *REINVENT* is an essential guide to not only mastering technology but also to mastering business in the 21st Century."

—DR. ERIC J. HOLSAPPLE, entrepreneur and author of *Profit with Presence*

"Modern businesses must navigate an unprecedented pace of change. And it's just going to keep accelerating—exponential innovations in technology mean we will likely see more change in the next 10 years than in the past 100. Look no further than ChatGPT shocking the world at the end of 2022. Any company that wants to survive must master digital transformation. With *REINVENT*, Faisal Hoque gives leaders a blueprint to guide them in the momentous but necessary task of making transformation a core business competency—including how leaders need to overhaul their own mindsets and behaviors."

—LARRY ENGLISH, CEO, Centric Consulting and *Forbes* contributor

"Author Faisal Hoque draws from his deep knowledge and extensive research to show how business digital transformation is not an option; it's a requirement driven by humans to enhance both employee and customer experiences. *REINVENT* addresses two critical challenges for digital transformation: First, an organization's leaders must be the driving force for meaningful digital improvements. Leaders must engage their workforce to create digital strategy and a participative culture to support transformational processes, priorities, and new ways of thinking, acting, and serving. Second, and building on this human element, *REINVENT* reassures readers that through a process of shared learning, investigation, review, and managing technology and business as 'one,' digital transformation can continually evolve to focus on an organization's most important priorities—and not become a static, panacea solution doomed to fail!"

—**CAROL A. POORE, PHD,** author of *Leadership in the Metaverse* and *Strategic Impact*

REINVENT

NAVIGATING BUSINESS TRANSFORMATION
IN A HYPERDIGITAL ERA

FAISAL HOQUE

FAST
COMPANY
Press

Fast Company Press
New York, New York
www.fastcompanypress.com

This work is being published under the Fast Company Press imprint by an exclusive arrangement with *Fast Company*. *Fast Company* and the *Fast Company* logo are registered trademarks of Mansueto Ventures, LLC. The Fast Company Press logo is a wholly owned trademark of Mansueto Ventures, LLC.

Distributed by Greenleaf Book Group

For ordering information or special discounts for bulk purchases, please contact Greenleaf Book Group at PO Box 91869, Austin, TX 78709, 512.891.6100.

Design and composition by Greenleaf Book Group and Sheila Parr
Cover design by Greenleaf Book Group and Sheila Parr
Cover image used under license from ©Alamy / Jirjis Nailul

Publisher's Cataloging-in-Publication data is available.

Print ISBN: 978-1-63908-042-7

eBook ISBN: 978-1-63908-044-1

To offset the number of trees consumed in the printing of our books, Greenleaf donates a portion of the proceeds from each printing to the Arbor Day Foundation. Greenleaf Book Group has replaced over 50,000 trees since 2007.

Printed in the United States of America on acid-free paper

23 24 25 26 27 28 29 30   10 9 8 7 6 5 4 3 2 1

First Edition

To Chris,

In our ever-changing world, you have been my constant anchor . . .

From the very beginning, now for more than three decades,
you have been rooting for me unconditionally.

You encouraged, inspired, and reassured me with heart, soul, and head—
elements that allowed me to repeatedly reinvent myself.

This is for you and the readers . . .

May your next chapter be full of meaningful impact and joy.

"The enterprise that does not innovate ages and declines, and in a period of rapid change such as the present, the decline will be fast."

—*Peter Drucker*

CONTENTS

FOREWORD

IF YOU'RE LOOKING FOR a top-notch expert in transformation who's been working in that field for a very long time, look no further . . . you've found your source.

Over the last twenty years, I have been watching Faisal's writing, impact, and recognition go from strength to strength. The book you are about to read, written at the apex of his career, represents a culmination of years of his research, practice, and reflection. You're in for a treat!

Just to put things in perspective. I still vividly remember a book on e-commerce—*e-Enterprise* (Cambridge University Press), which Faisal authored in the early 2000s, just as I was becoming a faculty member at Stanford's Graduate School of Business. Since then, Faisal has been publishing or co-authoring a book every two years, each one carefully helping senior leaders drive transformation through technology for maximum business impact. It came as no surprise to me when these books started winning awards and becoming *Wall Street Journal, USA Today,* Amazon, and Barnes and Noble best sellers. In between books, Faisal continued to address how we think about transformation through his writing with *Fast Company* and *Business Insider.*

REINVENT takes you on an all-inclusive, comprehensive, and practical journey to help you drive and accelerate your company's digital transformation. I use "all-inclusive" here intentionally to underscore just how thorough Faisal's analysis is. Case in point—most of us would argue that digital transformation is simply a business strategy requirement, or a competitive necessity. Faisal takes it to the next level by showing us how important digital transformation is if we want to attract and retain top tier talent. He also examines how digital transformation supports organizational security and keeps unwanted intruders at bay.

Then comes the "comprehensive" part. *REINVENT* takes us through every single step involved in digital transformation. He's seen organizations that get it right and those that don't. He discusses the importance of stakeholder management, culture, and leadership. In my own experience of helping large companies implement digital transformation, these three factors essentially make or break the entire effort. They pay huge dividends—as you'll see in your own transformation.

And finally, the "practical." Here, Faisal offers the acronym LIFTS (Learn, Investigate, Formulate, Take Off, and Study) as your ready-to-use framework for experimenting and scaling up your transformation. You'll use LIFTS, over and over, until it becomes ingrained in everything you do. It's a core element of your transformation.

As I said, you've come to the right place. And with that, I leave you to start your own reinvention journey!

—**Misiek Piskorski**
dean of IMD Asia and Oceania
professor of digital strategy, analytics, and
innovation, IMD Business School

PREFACE

ANYONE WHO BELIEVES THAT toys are strictly child's play need only look at Hasbro.

The company has been a mainstay in the toys and games industry since its founding in 1923. And for much of that time, Hasbro's focus was on the proverbial end user—the children themselves playing with My Little Pony and G.I. Joe figures.

But all that changed in 2012. Rather than marketing to children, the company shifted its focus to parents. Leveraging large-scale, data-driven efforts culled from and supported by an extensive social media presence, Hasbro concentrated its pitch on suggesting suitable games and toys, learning opportunities, and other like strategies—all of which was music to parents' ears. Further, it expanded the means through which all those fun items could be purchased, offering multiple retail channels in addition to traditional brick-and-mortar stores.

Admittedly, the technology and marketing budget needed to make all this happen carried a hefty price tag—Hasbro's marketing budget increased roughly tenfold. But the payoff was worth it and then some—sales grew by $1 billion, and the company's stock more than tripled in value.

Hasbro had effectively transformed itself, and that transformation was powered by digital technology capable of gathering and analyzing reams of valuable data, followed by the development of the strategies and systems with which to better reach and serve an exploding and changing marketplace.

A decidedly happy story. Unfortunately, it contrasts with an extensive list of digital transformation missteps and out-and-out failures.

Sportswear giant Nike is now a leader in digital business, but only after enduring an earlier failure at digital reinvention. In 2010, Nike launched a new business unit called Nike Digital Sport to support digital initiatives and create new technological capabilities across the company. Two years later, the firm released FuelBand, an innovative activity tracker.

The device was an initial hit with customers. The tracker could provide users with detailed statistics and helpful fitness guidance. It made Nike a trailblazer in wearable devices.

But it didn't last. For one thing, the company was unable to leverage all the valuable data and insight generated by FuelBand. Moreover, Nike couldn't find a sufficient number of engineers with appropriate technological training. Margins collapsed. By 2014, Nike had trimmed some 80 percent of its Digital Sport workforce.[1] Although the company has persevered and has enjoyed significant success through transformation.

Nike is by no means an outlier. According to some estimates, as many as 80 percent of business transformations that include a digital component fall short of expectations. That translates to an enormous cost. Recent research by the database company Couchbase found that companies wasted an average of $4.12 million per organization on failed, delayed, or scaled-back initiatives.[2]

And bear in mind, the report adds, that's something of an improvement.

Nike's experience might be seen as an idea before its time. After all, it's hard to spot a wrist these days without some gizmo monitoring heart rate, measuring steps, and collecting other sorts of data.

But the likely reasons are more complicated than that—and, sadly, more commonplace. Nike didn't have the technology in place to make the most of an enormous jump in data and analytic material. It couldn't track down the necessary talent—and those are merely the most cited issues.

How do savvy leaders such as those at Nike make these miscalculations to the tune of an 80 percent failure rate? Why do so many effectively pull the plug on multimillion-dollar efforts or settle for substandard returns?

That's the global challenge that this book aims to address.

Obviously enough, there are multiple factors that can contribute to a failed digital transformation. The economy is one such element—sometimes the timing is simply lousy enough to derail what might have otherwise been a successful reinvention.

But there's much more to it than mere luck. One obvious candidate for mismanagement is the distorted view many leaders have of technology—as an absolute savior that will correct everything else that's wrong with an organization. It can certainly help, but approaching it as a panacea is almost certainly a misstep.

Another source of failure lying in wait is the treatment of technology with a plug-and-play attitude. Buy it, install it, and off it goes—end of story. As many companies have discovered, to their discouragement, technology cannot even come close to its potential without constant attention to funding, personnel, evolution, and other factors. Moreover, technology must be closely aligned with a company's core mission, vision, culture, and strategic objectives. Otherwise, it can be doomed to the fate of a stand-alone disaster.

This one-dimensional consideration of technology provides clear indications of what might well be the most dangerous cause of all. Many leaders chronically fail to see—let alone appreciate—the absolute scope of what reinvention entails. Again, it's a mistake to see technology as a simple add-on. Rather, the implementation of digital technology carries ramifications throughout all areas of an organization. Leaders need to recognize that digital transformation isn't just going to change what you do—it's going to change how you think and act in profound ways, including adjustments to your culture, processes, priorities, and the very heart of your organizational strategy and direction.

How you think also impacts a transformation's timeline. Many mistakenly assume that transformation leveraging digital technology has an end point—you reach that particular step, and you're all done.

The truth is that transformation has no end of the line whatsoever. Given the rapid rate at which technology, the marketplace, and other elements are evolving and growing, it's ill-advised to see any technology—however cutting edge at the moment—as a definitive solution. It's going to keep changing and maturing—because it must.

But that's great news. Any organization that considers reinventing itself with a digital aspect is aware of the enormous potential—better decision-making, swifter adjustments to shifts in the marketplace, and far better methods of compiling and analyzing essential data, just to name several. Caveats notwithstanding, it's an appealing proposition—if not an outright necessity.

But it takes the right approach—practically, as well as emotionally and intellectually—to get there.

This book is divided into three distinct sections. The first section, "Why? The Case for Business Transformation in a Hyperdigital Era," makes the argument for organizational reinvention—from the changing nature of consumers to shifting workforce priorities to the necessity for greater organizational security.

The second section, "*Transformation* via Digitalization—Necessary Steps," examines actions necessary to prepare for transformation, including overcoming significant obstacles, recognizing the essential value of leadership, and forecasting what your organization is likely to become in the future.

The final section, "What to Do: Navigating with LIFTS," offers a comprehensive discussion of a five-step process geared to guiding your company through its transformation. Using the acronym LIFTS—learn, investigate, formulate, take off, and study—you'll learn what all goes into a successful transformative effort, including elements that, if overlooked, can sink otherwise solid planning.

As the statistics offered in this introduction affirm, organizational transformation with a digital component is a journey littered with land mines. Moreover, it's a journey that never reaches any sort of "destination." But not only is the journey worthwhile; it's absolutely essential to identify and respond to pervasive change in the marketplace, your competitors, and the overall character of the economy.

That takes both time and a willingness to approach things with a decidedly different mindset—yesterday's way of looking at your organization may as well be fifty years old, for all that it matters. Let's get started today with directing your attention toward tomorrow.

INTRODUCTION

MY JOURNEY WITH ORGANIZATIONAL transformation began more than twenty-five years ago. I have had the opportunity to work with a diverse group of public- and private-sector organizations, such as the U.S. Department of Defense, GE, MasterCard, American Express, Northrop Grumman, CACI, PepsiCo, IBM, Home Depot, Gartner, and JPMorgan Chase. I also have had the opportunity to develop more than twenty commercial business and technology platforms, along with launching, running, and growing several technology and business services companies.

In 2002, I wrote *The Alignment Effect: How to Get Real Business Value Out of Technology* (Financial Times). The cataclysmic end of the internet bubble signaled not only a stock implosion but also a dramatic *denouement* in what was actually a decade-long history of "technology for the sake of technology." This revelation and return to rational thinking seems self-evident: What leader, after all, would willingly throw millions of dollars at an investment without knowing how it could affect their business? If we use history as a guide to calculate the waste, the answer is an unpalatable "a lot." This was the premise of *The Alignment Effect*. In 2002, I also wrote a *Manager's Journal* article, "The Technology Disconnect," for the *Wall Street Journal*.

The Alignment Effect kicked off my lifelong journey to drive business and social value from technology from better leadership, management, and innovation. In 2004, I formed a cross-functional, cross-industry research think tank, called the Business Technology Management Institute, to enhance the management science of innovation and value creation from the use of technology. The institute created several best-practice management frameworks, maturity models, and indices in a very short order by leveraging real-life learning.

The institute published its seminal work, *Winning the 3-legged Race: When Business and Technology Run Together* (Prentice Hall), in 2005. Our hope was that it marked the beginning of a revolution in the management of business and technology together across the globe, and that what we were learning would not only benefit us all today but influence leaders of the future as well.

So many things have changed since then. I have traveled many miles, worked with a variety of talented innovators and leaders, and published other books on innovation, leadership, and the Fourth Industrial Revolution (4IR), including *Wall Street Journal* and *USA Today* best sellers *Everything Connects: Cultivating Mindfulness, Creativity, and Innovation for Long-Term Value* (2022, Fast Company Press) and *LIFT: Fostering the Leader in You Amid Revolutionary Global Change* (2022, Fast Company Press).

Given the rate of change that we have experienced and will continue to see, it's been a challenge trying to stay on top of everything that's taking place. Outside of constant technological evolution and growth, we've also been through a ghastly worldwide pandemic and increasing exposures to climate change that impacted not only people's physical and mental well-being but also the way we think about how we work, *why* we work, and other issues that influence us all—resulting in a completely reinvented playing field that only continues to change.

This entirely new environment can prove a steep climb for professionals and leaders looking to collaborate not only to build the sorts of businesses and organizations geared to leveraging change but also to create meaningful, long-term value. That's particularly tricky for existing organizations that must consider revising and possibly scrapping decades-old habits, processes, and their very ways of thinking and operating.

The promise inherent in new technologies can be one key to meeting these challenges. Although there are many variants, digital technology, at a high level, refers to electronic platforms, systems, devices, and resources that allow the storage, sharing, and analysis of an unprecedented amount of information and data. With these opportunities, organizations can literally reinvent themselves—not just in terms of what they're capable of doing and achieving but also in terms of how they can better position themselves to adapt and respond to all the change around them—with competitors, consumers, and the marketplace.

As we'll see, that will require much more than simply obtaining the latest technology, plugging it in, and sitting back to watch reinvention take place. From top to bottom, organizations will be compelled to change entire mindsets, attitudes, and assumptions about how they operate, how they can grow, and even the very reason for their existence. Change, as driven by technology, is as much an adjustment of mindset as it is a new set of tools that everyone must learn how to use.

This book is geared to addressing that unprecedented journey. And when I use the word *journey*, I mean to emphasize that reinvention never has any sort of fixed end point or conclusion. Rather, it's an ongoing pilgrimage—one characterized not only by obstacles to be met and overcome but also by fresh opportunities that are continually presented at each step along the journey.

But bear in mind that this is by no means a definitive manual that encapsulates all that you need to know about digital reinvention—no one book can do that. But what it can do is introduce you to ideas, concepts, and practical step-by-step strategies with which you can better position yourself and your organization to reap the greatest number of benefits that digital transformation can afford. It's a journey rich with promise.

But it can also be equally perilous. As you'll also learn, the road to transformation is complex, and several organizations and companies have failed to grasp the scope and import of what reinvention really encapsulates.

I believe this book will help you and your organization work toward realizing a far more rewarding and meaningful outcome.

SECTION 1

SECTION 1

WHY? THE CASE FOR BUSINESS TRANSFORMATION IN A HYPERDIGITAL ERA

BUSINESS TRANSFORMATION IS A ubiquitous phrase these days—and with good reason. From here onward, I will refer to business transformation as *Transformation*.

A confluence of factors and drivers—from exponential growth in the power and influence of technology to the impact of the COVID-19 pandemic and its varied iterations—has virtually reinvented the marketplace for nearly every type of business. That unto itself is a mandate for *Transformation*—a mandate I examine in more specific detail later in this section.

Transformation is a particularly apt term. When the market changes as quickly and completely as it has over just the past several years, organizations cannot respond with mere tweaks. Rather, *Transformation* is called for—a complete reworking that can include a thorough reorganization of people, processes, and the tools employed to carry out your business's mission.

And your organization should go beyond simple, minor adjustments to certainly include a digital component as well—the introduction of digital tools and capabilities that, if successful, will allow your organization to overcome the challenges and meet the demands of exponentially evolving markets.

Business transformation and digital transformation are essentially two separate ideas, but their close connection and synergy are undeniable. Further, any attempt at *Transformation* that lacks a significant digital presence might be compared with push-button phones that dial a split second faster—the best of intentions, but grossly outdated.

CHAPTER 1

YOUR CUSTOMER ISN'T WHAT HE OR SHE USED TO BE

AN IMPORTANT FIRST STEP in recognizing the necessity of *Transformation* that also incorporates digital transformation is the stark reality that your customer simply isn't what he or she used to be, and further, that consumers are going to continue to change. Any business or organization that doesn't recognize this reality will be misdirected from the very outset of any intended *Transformation*.

THE FLIGHT TO ONLINE SHOPPING

It's no great epiphany to realize that the COVID-19 pandemic fueled consumers' interest in—and enthusiasm for—online shopping, nor is it shocking that any business whose *Transformation* doesn't incorporate a significant digital element likely risks alienating an enormous segment of the consumer population.

E-commerce was already growing rapidly before COVID-19 struck, but the pandemic served to drive even more consumers online, spending much more via digital portals and more frequently than ever before. By one estimate, the pandemic contributed an extra $218 billion to e-commerce's bottom line over the past two years. In 2020, COVID-19 added $102 billion in U.S. e-commerce, tacking on an additional $116 billion in 2021.[1]

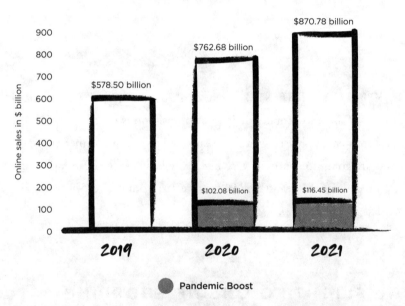

PANDEMIC ADDS TO U.S. E-COMMERCE SALES

Pandemic boost in sales as a portion of overall e-commerce sales

Figure 1.1. Pandemic adds extra $218.53 billion to U.S. e-commerce sales in 2020–2021.[2]

Additionally, what consumers are increasingly buying online continues to break new ground. Groceries and related home supplies are one such area. Online grocery sales increased 103 percent in 2020, with U.S. consumers spending $73.7 billion, according to an Adobe analysis. There wasn't a hint of slowdown in 2021 as consumers dropped $79.2 billion on online groceries. Further, Adobe anticipates spending to exceed $85 billion in 2022.[3]

The grocery category underscores a significant dynamic with regard to online consumer activity. During the initial phases of the pandemic—as well as the subsequent peaks and valleys that followed—the primary motivation for buying groceries online was clearly one of health and safety. That was particularly true prior to the development of COVID-19 vaccines—rather than risk their health to stock their pantries, consumers opted for the physical safety and security of online shopping.

The issue of health is still at play, but now it's far more a matter of speed and convenience. According to reports in *Supermarket News*, as the pandemic began to wane, only 27 percent of consumers ranked safety as most important. By contrast, 32 percent cited convenience as most important. One headline proclaimed, "Increased Use of Online Shopping 'Here To Stay.'"[4]

PRODUCT AVAILABILITY

What will be most important when shopping post–COVID-19?

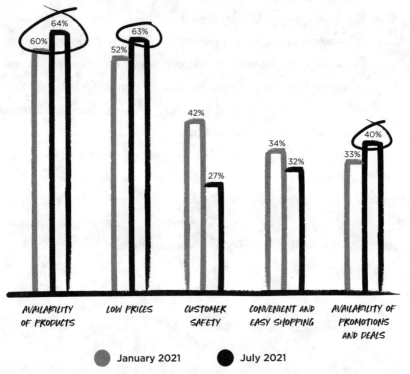

January 2021   July 2021

Figure 1.2. Product availability is still top of mind in addition to low prices and promotions.[5]

Significant growth is not only limited to food and drink. Prior to the pandemic, building supplier Lowe's had experienced rather anemic growth of online shopping—roughly 3 percent per year. But, anticipating the upcoming explosion of digital sales, Lowe's decided to remake much of the entire company, with digital at the core of that transformation. (Lowe's actually managed to introduce curbside pickup in a mere three days during the depths of the pandemic.) Digital-related purchases have soared as a result.

Further evidence of the continued explosion of online commerce is the eclectic—to put it mildly—array of items identified as particularly strong online sales candidates. According to the blog *Shopify*, they range from the usual suspects (e-books, computers, household cleaning supplies) to the retro (LPs and other forms of vinyl) to the frankly surprising (marine radar, DJ systems, and false eyelash accessories).[6]

The message is as understated as a meteor crashing to earth. Digital shopping is, indeed, here to stay. The pandemic may ebb, but not consumer enthusiasm for speed, efficiency, and convenience.

DIGITALLY ENABLED CONSUMERS ARE EMPOWERED LIKE NEVER BEFORE

The balance of power in any number of industries and markets has also been completely upended. Whereas the producers of goods and services once sat fairly and squarely in the driver's seat—you want it, we make it, you pay the price we specify—consumer muscle and influence have blossomed over the past few years. A number of factors are driving that complete change.

First is technology. Consumers are now capable of conducting almost limitless research into any buying decision, from rankings in consumer magazines to feedback from other consumers via online review venues. Social media itself affords consumers the opportunity to obtain insight and guidance from other customers across the globe.

This research capability is not limited to conventional yardsticks, such as product price, performance, and longevity. Consumers are increasingly coming to embrace other factors, such as a product or company's reputation in the community as a supportive, productive citizen. Consumers now value companies that do right by others, frequently relegating price to a somewhat secondary concern. Environmental impact and awareness are also considered.

Therein lies a significant reason why any effort at *Transformation* should include a digital presence. The first is, for better or worse, largely cosmetic. For many consumers, particularly younger ones, a mature digital presence is a sign of validation and legitimacy—any company that lacks an actionable online presence is often looked at skeptically. Whether fair or not, most of us have stopped to wonder—with a critical eye—why a particular business doesn't have a website or has obviously opted for a cheap, do-it-yourself version. Not very empirical, but we've all been there.

Additionally, a strong digital component can complement consumers' interest in product research. For example, a well-designed website that offers comprehensive information about a product or service is likely to resonate with consumers looking to conduct purchase homework. The longer you can compel a consumer to stay on your site and review what information you have to offer, the more you can meet a prospective customer's desire to be informed, and the better you can frame that knowledge to convince the customer that yours is the right buying choice.

Information, guidance, and advice also further the goal of appealing to consumer interest in a company's citizenship. By crafting websites that are easy to use and comprehensive in helping visitors research a particular product, a company portrays itself as a helpful, informative source—one geared toward educating customers and helping them make informed buying decisions.

A digital component can also make consumer research and buying that much more efficient. Self-service tools—such as how-to articles, instructional videos, and other features—allow consumers to better understand and troubleshoot issues without having to wait to engage with a live staff member (who is then free to tackle more involved issues and tasks).

A company is also enabled to effectively leverage growing consumer empowerment. For one thing, a digital presence allows a company to efficiently collect consumer feedback and suggestions—input that can be used not only to refine and improve products or services but also to strengthen the consumers' sense of influence and authority.

Taking this concept far enough can afford companies a variety of opportunities that compose customer co-creation. Co-creation refers to involving stakeholders—customers as well as employees—in addressing a particular problem or devising fresh solutions or products. This can include ideas such as new products, strategies to overcome delivery chain problems, or even technical solutions to complex manufacturing questions. The ultimate outcome results not only in products and services that better reflect the market but also in empowered consumers whose involvement enhances their roles as company and product advocates. Consumers have a clear hand in shaping the products and services they ultimately buy.

An ideal example is furniture manufacturer IKEA. In early 2018, IKEA launched co-createIKEA, a digital platform that urged customers and fans to participate in new product development. The overall program ranges from soliciting customer ideas to operating entrepreneurial "boot camps." Participants can receive cash prizes and, for designers and entrepreneurs, the opportunity to gain a valuable toehold in the world's largest furniture retailer.

Consumer empowerment is not limited to retail. Health care is another area where an increasing focus on consumer empowerment is expanding at a rapid rate. Patients now have unprecedented access to—and involvement in—their health-care decisions, from detailed cost breakdowns to readily available test results, treatments, and other components of their overall health-care programs.

More specifically, an increasing number of health-care providers are incorporating tools such as mobile apps, with which patients can better direct and understand their health care. Not only can such apps serve as a source of effective reminders for patients or their caregivers, but they can also boost patients' understanding of why they're taking a particular medication or following a specific treatment protocol. Over time, this results in more informed patients with a greater knowledge of what they personally can do to build better health. And, once again, the business or organization on the other end is seen as proactive, supportive, and community minded.

From health care to financial services, consumer knowledge and forms of participation are increasing at an exponentially exploding rate—a clear reflection of a growing recognition of how markets of all types are shifting to increasingly emphasize consumer involvement and impact. It's almost impossible to imagine such a scenario taking place without the influence and reach of a digital component. Even if such a level of consumer engagement would be possible in a relatively digital-free environment, it's almost certain that the entire process would be more unwieldy, cumbersome, and, as likely as not, far less appealing to consumers.

DIGITAL'S ROLE IN COMBATING SHIFTING CONSUMER LOYALTY

An old business axiom declares that it's far more expensive to attract new customers than it is to retain current customers. As the relationship between businesses and customers evolves at an ever-rapid pace, that bit of wisdom may be truer than ever.

Some three-quarters of American consumers say they've tried shopping in a different way in response to economic pressures, store closings, and changing priorities. This has shattered traditional brand loyalties, with 36 percent of consumers trying a new product brand. Of consumers who have tried different brands, 73 percent intend to continue to incorporate the new brands into their routine.[7]

Figure 1.3. *Seventy-five percent of consumers have tried a new shopping behavior, and most intend to continue it beyond the crisis.*[8]

Even more stark, those shifting loyalties are taking place at a more rapid pace than ever before. According to research by Accenture, more than three-quarters of consumers say they're changing their brand loyalty at a faster rate than only a few years ago. Moreover, many companies' efforts to retain consumer loyalty are failing, with nearly one-quarter of customers reporting a negative response to loyalty programs or—perhaps worse—no response at all.[9]

To make matters even more grim, tumbling loyalty rates mean more than simply losing any old customer. Compared to new customers, loyal customers bring higher returns, with 62 percent more likely to spend extra money on the brand and 59 percent more likely to choose the brand over competitors.

A *Transformation* that encompasses a digital role can prove effective in a variety of ways, from combating consumer flight to strengthening existing customer connections. For one thing, digitalization can boost the overall speed and positive experience of customer service, a key element to consumer loyalty. A full 69 percent of consumers in the United States reported that customer service is "very important" in their choice of—or loyalty to—a brand.[10]

Digitalization also creates a more personal customer experience. Services such as product recommendations, notifications of exclusive short-term sales, and other such features enable much closer and ongoing consumer contact. Additionally, consumers are that much more willing to share personal information about themselves—given assurances of systems and policies to ensure security—if, in return, they can participate in loyalty programs and other such offerings that "less loyal" customers might not be aware of.

Therein lies yet another digital advantage when it comes to addressing consumer loyalty. Given that consumers who feel amply compensated are particularly comfortable with passing along information about demographics, buying habits, and other pertinent information, a digital component attains much faster, more complete, and, ultimately, more useful insights into what customers need and value. That, in effect, completes a valuable circle—a digital component that boosts customer loyalty and, in turn, uncovers information with which that loyalty can be strengthened and expanded.

THE CONSUMER POPULATION—MORE DIVERSE, LESS DIVIDED, BUT FURTHER APART

The case for *Transformation* incorporating a meaningful digital component is further strengthened when examining the specifics of consumers themselves. Simply put, the demographics of almost every market are shifting. But that doesn't necessarily refer only to the makeup of consumers themselves, although they are, indeed, different from their predecessors. What has also shifted is the overall competitive environment and the options available to this different group.

One of the most significant shifts taking place with consumers is their overall diversity. Millennials—those born approximately between 1981 and 1994 and who now compose roughly 30 percent of the population—are unto themselves the most diverse generation in U.S. history, with ethnic and racial minorities making up approximately 44 percent. In contrast, a mere one-quarter of Baby Boomers—those born approximately between 1946 and 1964—consist of racial and ethnic minorities.[11]

Further, it is the Millennials who are leading the digitalization charge. Estimates suggest that Millennials (approximately 28–41 years old) make as much as 60 percent of their purchases online.[12] Perhaps even more significant, despite their relatively young age, is that 60 percent of Millennials report they have had a relationship with a specific brand for more than ten years—a powerful antidote to overall shaky consumer loyalty (and further cause for a top-tier digital presence).[13]

But the overall shift also undermines the commonly held assumption that younger consumers are exclusive in their adoption of online shopping. Fueled in large part by the COVID-19 pandemic, Baby Boomers aged 65 and older are now the fastest-growing group of online buyers, spending 49 percent more on the web in 2020 than they did the year prior.[14] Apparently, the "digital divide" isn't quite as cavernous as many of us had been led to believe—at least in this respect.

Nor is the evolving consumer base, which isn't limited to shifts among age groups. Overall, the non-Hispanic white population is projected to drop from 199 million in 2020 to 179 million in 2060—a 10 percent decline—even as the U.S. population continues to grow. This more heterogeneous consumer base will likely have a much broader and varied set of priorities and requirements.[15]

But for all the apparent inclusiveness of digitalization and online consumer activity, more global shifts are also impacting consumer demographics. While the digital divide may not necessarily apply to Boomers and their younger counterparts, there is a growing divide between the highest-income earners and others. Between 2007 and 2017, U.S. income growth for the highest earners (greater than $100,000 in mean household income) rose 1,305 percent more than the lower-income group (less than $50,000 in mean household income). Particularly stark is news that the bottom 40 percent of earners had less discretionary income in 2017 than they did ten years ago, with the next 40 percent enjoying only a minor increase.[16]

Taking that information a step further, it's reasonable to conclude that affluent urban consumers are the most likely to be predominantly online shoppers. According to a study by the National Retail Federation, 53 percent of study participants earning $75,000 or more described themselves as predominantly online shoppers. Additionally, 33 percent of those consumers also were likely to subscribe to an online delivery service such as Blue Apron or Birchbox.[17]

ONLINE VS. IN-STORE SHOPPERS

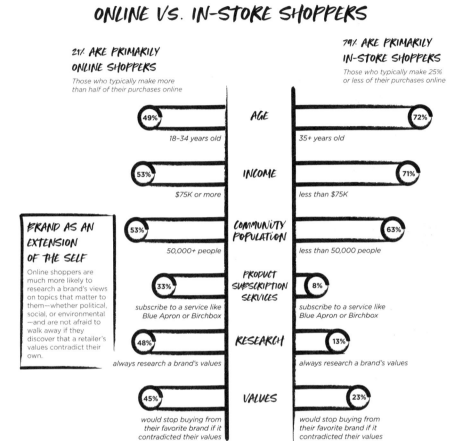

21% ARE PRIMARILY ONLINE SHOPPERS
Those who typically make more than half of their purchases online

79% ARE PRIMARILY IN-STORE SHOPPERS
Those who typically make 25% or less of their purchases online

	ONLINE	IN-STORE
AGE	49% — 18-34 years old	72% — 35+ years old
INCOME	53% — $75K or more	71% — less than $75K
COMMUNITY POPULATION	53% — 50,000+ people	63% — less than 50,000 people
PRODUCT SUBSCRIPTION SERVICES	33% — subscribe to a service like Blue Apron or Birchbox	8% — subscribe to a service like Blue Apron or Birchbox
RESEARCH	48% — always research a brand's values	13% — always research a brand's values
VALUES	45% — would stop buying from their favorite brand if it contradicted their values	23% — would stop buying from their favorite brand if it contradicted their values

BRAND AS AN EXTENSION OF THE SELF

Online shoppers are much more likely to research a brand's views on topics that matter to them—whether political, social, or environmental—and are not afraid to walk away if they discover that a retailer's values contradict their own.

Figure 1.4. *Differences between online and in-store shoppers.*[18]

Overall, the shifting makeup, habits, and preferences of the consumer population put together a compelling argument for *Transformation* that includes a significant digital role. In many ways, today's consumers are not so much changed as they are completely reinvented. Any business or organization that misses this essential point and, as a result, fails to transform itself adequately will be left in the digital dust.

NEED TO KNOW:

- Customers have changed drastically in recent years. They're more demanding and expect their feedback to be taken into consideration.
- The COVID-19 pandemic merely provided additional impetus to move to online shopping.
- Customer co-creation—where customers have a direct hand in developing new products—is increasing.
- The internet's ability to offer comprehensive comparison shopping is compromising consumer loyalty.

CHAPTER 2

YOUR WORKFORCE IS CALLING
FOR *TRANSFORMATION*

TAKING NOTHING AWAY FROM the exploding influence exerted by consumers, they are anything but alone in advocating for *Transformation* with a digital component. Your employees, contractors, and anyone else with whom you work are likely every bit as vocal.

Moreover, that advocacy isn't coming in the form of a polite request. As the past year has shown, talented professionals are voting with their feet, essentially refusing to endure what they deem as unacceptable—be that their work, the work environment, or some other amalgam of dissatisfaction.

In its own way, the "Great Resignation" has underscored a longstanding lack of attention to a central component of operating a successful organization. On the one hand, there are likely few, if any, business leaders who fail to emphasize the value of the customer experience. But, as the resignation seems to reveal, relatively few assign the same priority to the experience of employees.

And that's where much of the opportunity of the Great Resignation lies. By transforming a business and incorporating a meaningful digital element, business leaders have the means at hand not only to boost the customer experience but also to concurrently recraft the employee experience.

THE GREAT REEVALUATION

For fans of Western movies, the largest stampede ever captured on film has nothing whatsoever on what has been labeled as the Great Resignation.

The pandemic-era phenomenon has seen millions of employees voluntarily leaving their jobs. In January 2022 alone, some 4.3 million workers quit, adding to the staggering 48 million who abandoned their jobs in 2021, according to federal data.[1]

Ask ten experts for the reason behind this massive migration, and you'll probably get twice as many answers. But, as reported in a Joblist survey, several common elements stand out. For one thing, roughly 19 percent of people who took part in the study didn't like how their bosses treated them during the pandemic, 17 percent left due to inadequate benefits, and an additional 13 percent said they lacked a viable work-life balance.[2]

Although other factors certainly played a role, taken together, the Great Resignation embodies a reevaluation on the part of millions—rethinking their careers, long-term goals, work environments, and how to strike a healthier balance between work and play. However unsettling and disruptive the employee exodus has been, it also highlights the enormous need and opportunity for companies of all types to transform every aspect of their organizations.

Those organizations that leverage that opportunity as much as possible—including incorporating digital technology—will not only be better positioned to address employee satisfaction proactively but also be better able to adjust and respond to the constantly shifting marketplace of the future. Those who do not will simply struggle to survive—often, unsuccessfully.

AN INCREASINGLY REMOTE WORKFORCE—A RECASTING OF THE OFFICE

It's difficult to imagine anyone remembering any aspect of the COVID-19 pandemic with fondness. But, if such a thing existed, it might well be the pandemic's impact on where people carried out their work responsibilities.

When work shifted to a remote setting for many employers in early 2020, many companies understandably assumed the situation would be temporary at most—that most people would be back on-site within a few months.

As we now know, that's hardly been the case. For one thing, those few months have stretched out to years. Moreover, a substantial chunk of the working population found that they enjoyed working away from a conventional office setting, at least part of the time.

Studies substantiate that conclusion. In its first "State of Remote Work" survey, released in late 2021, the background check provider GoodHire found that 68 percent of employees would rather work from home. That attitude seems anything but fleeting or hollow—nearly half of respondents said they'd either quit their job or search for a new one that offered remote work benefits if their employer ordered them to return to the office. Further, many employees expressed a willingness to take a pay cut or forfeit certain benefits in exchange for a remote work option.[3]

Their enthusiasm is well justified. In one respect, studies have found that remote work, even for part of the time, has helped many employees establish a healthier work-life balance—one core reason for the tsunami of employees leaving their jobs throughout the Great Resignation. Additionally, the absence of downtime during commutes not only contributes to greater employee productivity but also helps address many of the health issues associated with the stress of commuting, including higher cholesterol and blood sugar levels, increased risk of depression, and other mental health issues.

Despite overwhelming evidence that many employees clearly want the option of a more flexible work arrangement, a discouraging number of employers are hesitant to adapt. According to the study "Strategies for Talent Engagement in the Reimagined Workplace," a full 25 percent of employers are planning on having employees return to a full-time, conventional, in-house work setting.[4] Others put the percentage at a much higher level—in an early 2022 survey by Microsoft, a full 50 percent of employers wanted their people to return to the office five days a week.[5] (Small wonder that, in the "Reimagined Workplace" study, more than one-third of employees felt that management was not sufficiently empathetic to their needs.)

The reasons for this insistence on trying to "return to normal" are varied. One commonly cited argument is that company culture cannot be maintained adequately if workers are consistently scattered. (A popular tweet in response showed a dismal, empty work cubicle with the introduction: "The culture.")[6]

As it happens, the precise opposite is true. A study by the research firm Gartner—which encompassed some 5,000 employees—found that incorporating remote work and a hybrid model that included both on-site and remote work significantly boosted employee engagement and sense of inclusion.[7] The reason is hard to miss—management that recognizes a desire from employees for more flexibility in work arrangements is bound to bolster a more positive, constructive culture.

Another apparent reason for the disconnect between employers and employees is the disparity of experience. As some observers have pointed out, a more highly paid executive is likely to enjoy such benefits as a private office, solitude, and privacy that their cubicle-bound colleagues may only experience now and then. Given a higher pay scale, those in management likely don't endure the financial hardship of childcare as do their lesser-paid colleagues. In short, the impact of being able to work from home is probably less meaningful to them—if even recognizable.

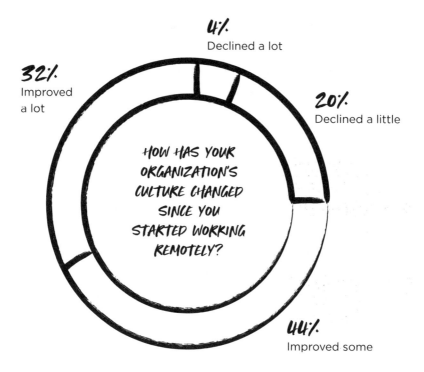

CULTURE CHANGE

4%
Declined a lot

32%
Improved
a lot

20%
Declined a little

HOW HAS YOUR ORGANIZATION'S CULTURE CHANGED SINCE YOU STARTED WORKING REMOTELY?

44%
Improved some

n = 1,750 newly remote or hybrid employees who report organizational culture
has changed since they started to work remotely
© 2021 Gartner, Inc. All rights reserved. CTMKT_1139941

Figure 2.1. Culture change with shift to remote work is mostly seen as positive.[8]

Perhaps a more applicable criticism of remote work is that it can lead to a sense of isolation among certain employees. A Gensler Research Institute survey found that what respondents missed most about being in an office was the people, specifically meeting and socializing with colleagues, "impromptu face-to-face time," and being a part of the office community."[9] That observation is borne out by research, one example of which found that seven out of ten employees felt more isolated after switching to remote work.[10] Others have noted that the sense of isolation has been bolstered by COVID-19's capacity to disrupt the sense of belonging that a physical office can offer.

(The issue of loneliness has prompted several companies and websites to offer what—audibly at least—might be the next best thing. There are now apps and websites that replicate the ambient sounds of an office, from footsteps and subdued chatter to the ringing of phones—and even the occasional *whoosh* of a flushing toilet.)

Obviously, something has to give. And *Transformation*, in which digitalization plays a central role, can be key to leveraging the advantages of remote work arrangements while addressing the drawbacks.

As for those downsides, *Transformation* should also include management's initiative to help remote workers address and mitigate the issues of isolation and loneliness. And that has nothing whatsoever to do with technology.

While tools such as video conferencing and other similar technology can help bridge the physical separation of remote work, it's incumbent that management implement steps to help employees learn how to best work from a remote setting. Rather than simply letting remote employees find strategies on their own, leaders can help enormously by proactively researching and implementing instructional programs with which remote workers can understand how to best navigate a remote work lifestyle. There are several actions management may take:

- Encourage remote workers to avoid working from home exclusively. Whether suggesting that off-site workers come to the office on a regular basis or work at least one day a week outside the home, such as in a coffee shop, leaders can beat loneliness to the punch by advocating a variety of alternative work settings. Phrased another way, remote doesn't have to mean just working at home.

- Urge remote workers to unplug. A commonly cited social issue of remote work is the feeling of never being able to get away from work. Combat that with a routine that specifies when work ends, such as a certain time of day when emails can go unread or an office door that is closed and left behind.

- Establish a broad network—and don't just talk about work. Encourage remote employees to interact with people other than those with whom they work. Moreover, don't limit conversations with colleagues to work matters. As they might likely do in the office, make it a point to bring up other topics.

- Leverage the flexibility. With regard to social matters, make certain that remote workers use their more flexible schedules for issues beyond work. Have some downtime during the day? Take Rover for a walk, start dinner, or do a few minutes of gardening. Don't treat the idea of shutting down your laptop thirty minutes earlier than you usually do as professional blasphemy.

- Take the time to remind remote workers they're an important part of a team. Be proactive in soliciting input and feedback from remote workers: What can you do on your end to make their lives better? What might they suggest to others who may be newcomers to remote work? Routinely ask them what they would do differently to strengthen the remote work experience.

When it comes to the well-being of remote workers, *Transformation* encompasses more than new technology or redesigned business practices. It also means recognizing that remote work, for all its advantages, does have its caveats. That balanced perspective can go a long way in making the most of remote work's potential—not to mention digitalization's possibilities for all employees, remote or otherwise.

THEY WANT MORE FLEXIBILITY—
WHETHER YOU LIKE IT OR NOT

Although the reasons for the Great Resignation are wide and varied, one issue at the heart of what employees value is greater flexibility. Any sweeping form of *Transformation* that fails to address that desire will miss an essential target.

Perhaps even more concerning, leaders often fail to realize just how important genuine flexibility is—so much so that their view of flexibility can differ substantially from that of their workforce.

Likely in large part from having experienced greater professional flexibility during COVID-19, a significant proportion of employees wants to hang on to that aspect of pandemic life. In fact, in one study, a striking 79 percent of professionals want to maintain their newfound flexibility post-pandemic.[11]

Unfortunately, this is where a significant disconnect kicks in. The 2021 Gartner Hybrid Work Employee Survey of 4,000 employees found that roughly three-quarters of executive leaders believe they have an established culture of flexibility. By contrast, only 57 percent of employees believe that their employers truly embrace flexible work. Further, nearly three-quarters of executives believe the business understands how flexible work patterns support employees; only half of employees share this view.[12]

That's a chasm that needs to be narrowed. And *Transformation*, which includes a significant digital role, can help.

In addition to other positive elements, many employees embrace remote work because of the inherent flexibility—the capacity to work in a variety of locations, on a number of different projects and activities, and at times that complement other areas of their lives. With digital transformation, businesses can address all three aspects of flexibility.

Further, it reinforces the validity of any type of *Transformation*—when looking to reinvent any organization, it's critical to start with people first.

Any form of change that prioritizes other elements—such as technology—may seem transformative, but it is almost certainly doomed to failure, or at the very least, to producing a reinvention that fails to accomplish all that it could have.

The reason is obvious. The only change that truly works in any organization is change that betters the experience of people. And digitalization can help cement a commitment to flexibility—a cornerstone of employees' view of an engaging and supportive place to work.

A TRANSFORMED, DIGITAL ORGANIZATION ENJOYS BETTER COMMUNICATION AND INNOVATION

The prior section addressing flexibility also touches on another core element of *Transformation* coupled with digitalization—better communication.

As the issue of flexibility illustrates, management and others within an organization are often miles apart when it comes to communication. Perhaps the organization lacks adequate means with which to communicate; alternatively, stakeholders may merely assume they know what everyone else believes or values. On a more extreme level, it's occasionally an issue where management simply isn't interested in what others have to say.

Although the last reason is surely a fuse just waiting for a spark, the two prior reasons and others similar to them are both understandable and correctable—tasks that a digital workplace can address effectively.

A digital workplace naturally encourages two-way communication between lower-level and higher-level employees to strengthen a free-flowing exchange of ideas within an organization. Social intranet programs such as LumApps and Simpplr are designed to encourage idea sharing and brainstorming at all levels. Tools such as interactive surveys, immediate feedback channels, and other ways to support collaborative capacity provide a means of connecting and interaction that is always available—unlike meetings and "huddles," which have to be announced and physically coordinated.

A transformed environment including digitalization can also bolster innovation. This is yet another area where traditional thinking and reality can butt heads. To innovate, according to longstanding practice, it's imperative to physically bring people together to exchange ideas, offer feedback, and both encourage and critique.

That's true to a certain degree but not to the extent that proponents believe. A physical gathering, while often energizing, can also inadvertently strengthen compliance. Consider a room with ten people, nine of whom are on board with a particular idea. It may happen completely innocently, but it's hard to deny the pressure that can potentially be placed on the remaining one who has a different idea.

Digitalization can address these and other stumbling blocks. For one thing, a digital network increases ready inclusion of everyone in an organization, providing greater diversity of ideas. Additionally, innovation can take place at a much faster rate—people can share ideas when a thought occurs to them, rather than having to wait for an appropriate physical setting. That's particularly critical moving forward, as the onus to introduce new products and services faster while also adjusting on the fly will prove critical to success.

Finally, a move away from physical settings can mitigate a tendency toward *group think*. As Brian Elliott, executive leader of the Future Forum (a research group formed by the workplace-messaging platform Slack), noted, traditional brainstorm sessions can push participants' thinking toward needless conformity.

Elliott said, "The truth is, whiteboarding leads to group think. If you allow people to submit ideas on their own, not in a room with others, studies show you'll get more creativity."[13]

A TRANSFORMED DIGITAL WORKFORCE IS MORE PRODUCTIVE AND COST-EFFICIENT

The reasons behind the appeal of a transformed, digital-current workplace for employees are both varied and powerful. But employees are not the only ones who stand to benefit from a reinvented and technologically sound environment—the rewards for the organization itself can also be significant.

With a growing proportion of employees working remotely at least part of the time, technology is becoming increasingly essential to ensure off-site personnel remain connected and engaged with their colleagues. But technology isn't limited to merely staying in touch—the right tools can also be leveraged to boost workplace productivity, no matter the overall physical logistics.

The challenge is something of a double-edged sword. Varied forms of technology allow higher levels of ongoing interaction, collaboration, and information sharing. But at the same time, imagine an employee's workstation with 100 new emails in the inbox, fifteen tabs open in a browser, and texts coming in like a tsunami wave on his or her cell phone. It's akin to the popular employee with whom everyone enjoys talking. As the visits to the cubicle never seem to end, so too does work languish on the desk without sufficient time to complete it.

That makes productivity tools essential to keeping things moving forward. Taking in everything from project management to collaboration to simply better management of work time, such tools can help better organize the greater flow of material and information that a technologically current work environment can involve. And that goes for on-site personnel as well as a colleague working from home in a bathrobe.

In addition to producing better organized information, productivity tools can also accelerate results. Technology affords leaders the opportunity to rejigger work processes from the ground up, with an ample dose of automated systems that further speed up the overall process. The result is a greater number of employees accomplishing more in less time.

Even better, such tools can further leverage an established truth regarding off-site employees—they're likely to be more productive to begin with than their in-office counterparts.

One survey by cloud provider CoSo Cloud found more than three-quarters of remote workers reporting higher productivity levels.[14] The study attributed much of that increase to digital tools optimizing work processes and, as a result, reducing work time. Anecdotally, it's also not hard to imagine that a remote worker, extracted from an office setting riddled with distractions, simply has the opportunity for more focused work.

And, happily, these factors can add up to a healthier bottom line. According to digital workplace research by Avanade, an internet consulting service provider, organizations have seen a 43 percent increase in revenue by implementing digital workplaces.[15] Not only can this be attributed to higher rates of overall productivity and efficiency, but other attendant expenses, such as reduced office maintenance, equipment, travel expenses, and other outlays, also contribute to lower costs.

IF YOU BUILD IT, THEY WILL COME (AND STAY)

As the Great Resignation underscored, keeping employees happy and engaged now mandates more than just complimentary bagels and arcade games in the break room. Top talent now essentially demands that a work environment be engaging, flexible, and geared toward professional development.

That translates to a reimagined work setting equipped with sufficient digital capability to address all those priorities.

In terms of attracting top talent, a digitally current work environment creates broadened work settings that qualified professionals seek. According to a study by DailyPay, a financial software developer, 56 percent of potential employees said companies that offer the ability to work remotely are more attractive to them when they're looking for work.[16] As more companies look to boost their digital capability moving forward, top-tier talent focused on their professional growth are certain to be attracted to firms that recognize digital's growing value.

Digital's role in helping to build a more diverse workforce is another plus. Using digital's capabilities, such as leveraging social media to broaden brand recognition, digitally focused strategies allow companies to connect with a larger, more diverse potential work pool. And, say those potential candidates, a work setting that is more inclusive and incorporates different backgrounds and perspectives is far more desirable than a stratified environment.

Digital can also help with the recruiting process itself. For one thing, by maintaining an active and vibrant presence on social media, a company can attract interest from potential employees, whether there happen to be current openings or not. In effect, digital allows organizations to build a talent pool well before any staffing needs emerge.

Digital capability can also help identify skills that are in increasing demand. By using quantitative data from aptitude tests, as well as more qualitative information such as a candidate's way of speaking and behavior, organizations can pinpoint candidates with "soft skills," such as the ability to communicate and to empathize with others, early in the recruiting process. Similarly, onboarding processes can also be improved and strengthened through tools such as online tutorials that allow new hires to learn policies, procedures, and other information before beginning work, rather than a more traditional induction event, which can often pack in far too many details to be of genuine benefit.

Many of the factors that boost an organization's appeal to potential candidates—remote work alternatives, greater flexibility, and diversity, just to name a few—also contribute to strengthened retention rates. Companies that have adopted a digital workplace have experienced a 25 percent lower turnover rate, according to one source.[17] The dynamic is obvious—a digitally current company not only appeals to the best, most suitable talent available but, by maintaining digital capabilities at a higher level, also provides the sort of professional growth opportunities that top-tier talent wants to stick with.

AN IMPROVED CUSTOMER EXPERIENCE

The benefits of *Transformation* and digital growth aren't confined to your organization and the people who compose it. Customers and clients are on the receiving end as well. Several studies have shown that an improved employee experience contributes to a better customer experience.

A July survey by research firm International Data Corporation (IDC) showed that happier, more engaged employees translate into a better customer experience and higher customer satisfaction. More specifically, 62 percent of survey respondents believed that there is a defined causal relationship between employee and customer experience—further, they deemed the connection both substantial and measurable.[18]

That's not just a reflection of greater motivation and productivity. As suggested by the IDC research, employees with a stronger work-life balance who feel they are being heard and are given the tools to do their work efficiently become stronger brand advocates. As a result, they simply care more about what they do, a vibe that translates into happier, more loyal customers. In that same research, nearly six out of ten participants said customer satisfaction was a central component in determining employee productivity.

It's clear that great employee experiences translate into great consumer experiences. Professionals on the hunt for such an experience are increasingly finding it in companies that have transformed themselves from soup to nuts—including a significant digital role.

NEED TO KNOW:

- Not only are remote working arrangements increasing, but employees are also taking them into consideration when choosing for whom they will work.
- Rather than distancing employees, research has found that remote work options have improved employee engagement.
- When considering remote work, it's essential to consider the issue of isolation and to develop strategies to counter it.
- Digitalization can promote efficiency, greater creativity, and innovation, not to mention increased organization productivity.

CHAPTER 3

SECURITY IS ALSO CHANGING— TRANSFORMING THE SAFETY OF YOUR BUSINESS

TRANSFORMATION THAT SIMPLY DOESN'T go far enough—in terms of sufficient change of scope and impact—can fall short of the range of opportunities that complete reinvention can achieve. That's particularly true regarding the digital element of *Transformation* and the security of your business or organization because the very nature of security is changing—and by no means exclusively for the better.

Already addressed in earlier chapters, adding or updating the digital component of your business can afford great benefits, from healthier revenue to an organization that attracts and retains top talent. Work processes can become more efficient, people are genuinely engaged, and the logistics of work become more flexible as on-site and remote employees work together seamlessly.

But progress also carries significant caveats. The more digitalization takes hold of nearly every aspect of life, so too does the issue of security become that much more central. Threats of all sorts are increasing and diversifying at the same time, which mandates digital transformation be characterized by proactive measures and the highest possible security awareness. And as is addressed later in this chapter, that mandate goes well beyond the confines of your business, making digital security a priority for everyone.

THE DANGERS OF OUTDATED OR INADEQUATE SECURITY

Government, business, and society are relying increasingly on technology to manage everything from public services to business processes. As this migration into the digital universe continues and accelerates, the threats of cybercrime and security lapses of all descriptions loom large. The cost, while enormous from a financial standpoint, goes beyond monetary issues: infrastructure, societal stability, national security, and mental health—both group and individual—are also at risk.

If that seems like an overreaction, consider the issue from the most specific perspective possible. According to Javelin's 2020 Identity Fraud Study, roughly one in every twenty Americans are impacted by identity theft every year. Monetarily speaking, that translates to roughly $17 billion in fraud.[1]

IDENTITY THEFT

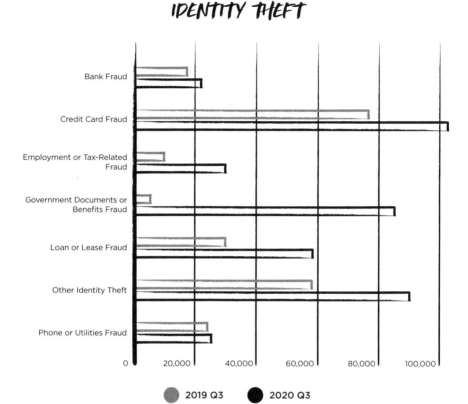

Figure 3.1. Identity theft reports across categories.[2]

Upping that scope just a bit, according to a recent report by IBM and the Ponemon Institute, the average cost of a data breach in 2021 in the United States was a shocking $4.24 million, and a 10 percent jump from the prior year.[3]

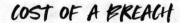

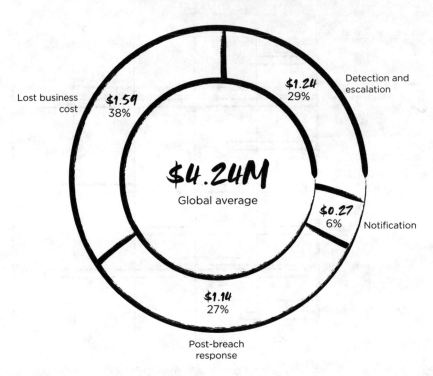

Figure 3.2. Average total cost of a breach divided into four categories.[4]

Security fails are particularly devastating to small businesses—an estimated 60 percent close within six months of being hacked.[5]

There are a variety of reasons why cybercrime is exploding exponentially. First is simply the reality that an array of entities, from small privately run businesses to expansive government agencies, are using digital-based systems more and more. And greater use means a broader variety of targets.

Further, from an entrepreneurial standpoint, the bad guys are also doing a terrific job of coming up with new ways and tools to compromise all sorts of digital systems and networks. In mid-April 2022, U.S.

officials announced the discovery of an alarmingly comprehensive and effective system for attacking industrial facilities—including the ability to cause explosions. Private security experts speculated it could take months or years to develop strong countermeasures.[6]

That's discouragingly consistent. While those with malicious intent are proving to be alarmingly innovative, those on the other side have simply failed to keep pace with means to fend off such increasing attacks—even to the point of neglecting to train an adequate number of people to join the fight. As detailed in the report "The Life and Times of Cybersecurity Professionals 2021," the Information Systems Security Association found nearly 100 percent agreement among respondents that the "cyber skills gap"—the number of people trained in cybersecurity—has not improved in the past five years.[7]

CYBERSECURITY SKILLS

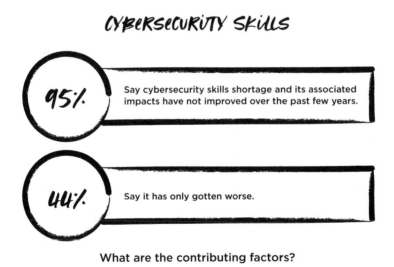

95% Say cybersecurity skills shortage and its associated impacts have not improved over the past few years.

44% Say it has only gotten worse.

What are the contributing factors?

Figure 3.3. Cybersecurity skills trends.[8]

Those and other problems are reflected in the increasing frequency and aggressiveness of cybercrime. One glaring example—faltering supply chains—became particularly evident during the COVID-19 pandemic. As has occurred in other areas of commerce, increasing digitalization of physical supply chains created new soft security points. Moreover, supply chains' reliance on technology providers and other third parties made them equally vulnerable. And it showed—in December 2021, just one week after discovering a critical security flaw in a widely used software library, the security company Check Point detected more than 100 attempts to exploit the vulnerability per minute.[9]

Another problematic issue is legal in nature. Simply put, there are few obstacles to getting into the ransomware racket. So-called cyber mercenaries are eager to provide access to sophisticated cyber-intrusion tools to facilitate a myriad of attacks. And once you're in the game, it's fairly easy to remain in it. Cryptocurrencies have allowed cybercriminals to collect payments with only modest risk of detection, prosecution, or monetary penalties.[10]

SHOCKS TO REFLECT UPON

NotPetya 2.0

What if an attack that is even more expansive and costly than the original NotPetya—with the ability to self-propagate and mutate to avoid preventative measures—created cascading lockups of systemically important businesses, thus bankrupting organizations, disrupting services, and unwinding the digital transformation efforts made over the past years?

Sovereignty slips

What if the shifts toward privately held technology infrastructure, as well as cryptocurrency and decentralized finance, undermine governments' control over data, processes, and financial systems?

Undetected disruption

What if subtle changes in health, banking, or other data go undetected for years but carry significant consequences for premature death, loss of funds, or other significant damages over time? How can cyber espionage compromise return on R&D investment and competitiveness in the future?

Figure 3.4. Shocks to reflect upon.[11]

Greater sophistication has also allowed cybercriminals to pick targets of choice, rather than simply settling for short-lived opportunities. This can allow cyberattacks to be carried out at highly specific points with a greater potential payback while still letting criminals capitalize on short-term opportunities, such as natural disasters.

Outdated forms of technology also allow for an array of ready targets—even those on a relatively small scale. For example, the information that passes electronically from a workstation to a printer can be readily attacked as hackers develop increasingly sophisticated tools for hijacking printer-bound data. Looked at another way, a system once seen as cutting edge and ultraconvenient can prove to be a vulnerable dinosaur to adept cybercriminals—yet another reason to ditch outdated tools in favor of digital platforms.

CONSEQUENCES FOR BUSINESSES

As cyber threats continue to multiply, so too do the risks and potential consequences for businesses of all types and sizes. First and most obvious is the financial threat. As cyberattacks grow in number, size, and complexity, businesses will likely be forced to pay increasingly large ransoms—that or suffer the operational, regulatory, and reputational mayhem that an effective cyberattack can carry out.

The consequences are also not limited to the primary target—vendors and supply chain partners can also be affected. Additionally, consider the overall financial fallout for a company that fails to adequately invest in cybersecurity protections. On the one hand, it can be subject to continued cyber blackmail. On the other, it may suffer even more should government regulators move to prohibit ransom payments. Even now, regulators can levy penalties on companies with inadequate digital safety precautions, such as investment houses.

Reputation is still another reason for concern. Since the consequences of cyberattacks are becoming increasingly well known, it's not difficult to imagine investors and venture capital firms backing away from a company that—whether through ignorance or delusional confidence—fails to take the self-protective steps that others see as absolutely essential. That's the sort of erosion of trust and confidence that can prove difficult, if not impossible, to rebuild.

Setting aside the devastating financial, operational, and reputational fallout of subpar technological protections, outdated technology can also prove a significant obstacle for companies that are genuinely interested in transforming themselves. In one respect, many legacy systems lack features necessary for digital reinvention. Further complicating matters are proprietary, specifically designed systems that are simply not open to upgrades. Those and other factors can leave the most well-intentioned businesses or organizations locked into their current systems and unable to afford the complete overhaul that outdated technology requires.

ENOUGH CAVEATS—THE PLUSES OF DIGITALIZATION

Any form of *Transformation* that lacks a significant and current digital component is like building the most beautiful home on a fault line. Sooner or later, unprotected beauty can be subject to disaster—that's particularly painful when, like consciously placing a mansion right above volatile earth, the danger was evident for all to see.

Luckily, *Transformation* incorporating digital advances can offer a variety of reliable protection. Playing off an example in the prior section, let's start with something as basic as possible—printed materials. Digital records are inherently more secure than traditional printed counterparts—a reality that many in leadership positions still fail to acknowledge.

Let's assume that an equally traditionally minded criminal is able to obtain sensitive printed information from your organization. Since the data is in straightforward printed form, the information they contain is easy to extract and leverage. The same thing can take place if printed material is lost or misplaced—material there for the taking may fall into the wrong hands.

Digital documentation is drastically different. Given that such data can be encrypted, it's no longer a matter of simply reading what you want to know. Granted, even encrypted material can be broken, given time and adequate resources, but it's certainly a far more difficult challenge than simply reading from a piece of paper—an important measure of protection, particularly for sensitive data.

The value of digitalizing records also makes a compelling argument against any sort of halfway transformative measure. It can be understandably tempting for many organizations—particularly those strapped for cash—to only partially digitize material and leave a portion in traditional printed form. For one thing, that can leave a significant amount of critical data open to theft. Further, management can become an ongoing headache as employees try to recall what material exists in digital form and what remains on paper.

Implicit in the greater amount of protection afforded by comprehensive digitalization is a business's increased capacity for resiliency. By committing sufficient resources to making digitalization a strong and vibrant component of any transformative effort, businesses naturally become better positioned to withstand future crises—and, just as important, emerge from them considerably more intact.

To that end, an executive survey from Deloitte suggests more "digitally mature companies"—companies where digital strategy and infrastructure are in place throughout every part of the business—are stronger and more agile in a crisis, from the havoc of Mother Nature to shifts in consumer and marketplace activity. Further, digitalization can improve product quality and customer satisfaction, thereby strengthening financial performance. Digitalization can also bolster social reputation by trimming environmental impact and increasing workforce diversity.[12]

DIGITAL MATURITY

DIGITAL PIVOT	DESCRIPTION
Flexible, secure infrastructure	Implementing technology infrastructure that balances security and privacy needs with the ability to flex capacity according to business demand
Data mastery	Aggregating, activating, and monetizing soiled, underutilized data by embedding it into products, services, and operations to increase efficiency, revenue growth, and customer engagement
Digitally savvy, open talent networks	Retooling training programs to focus on digital competencies, and staffing teams through flexible, contingent talent models to rapidly access in-demand skill sets and flex the organization's workforce based on business needs
Ecosystem engagement	Working with external business partners, including R&D organizations, technology incubators, and start-up companies, to gain access to resources such as technology, intellectual property, or people to increase the organization's ability to improve, innovate, and grow
Intelligent workflows	Implementing and continuously recalibrating processes that make the most of both human and technological capabilities to consistently produce positive outcomes and free up resources for higher-value actions
Unified customer experience	Delivering a seamless customer experience built around a 360-degree view of the customer that is shared company-wide so that customers experience coordinated digital and human interactions that are useful, enjoyable, and efficient in immersive, engaging environments
Business model adaptability	Expanding the organization's array of business models and revenue streams by optimizing each offering to adapt to changing market conditions and augment revenue and profitability

Figure 3.5. Seven digital pivots propel an organization's progress toward digital maturity.[13]

Digitalization can also address the ongoing challenge of maintaining and protecting reliable supply chains—a challenge made all the more daunting by COVID-19. Since the start of the pandemic, a reported

94 percent of Fortune 1,000 companies have experienced supply chain disruptions. Additionally, as the world begins to reopen post-pandemic, companies are scrambling to catch up as demand returns to pre–COVID-19 levels.[14]

A rare "positive" consequence of the COVID-19 pandemic highlighted widespread inefficiencies and lack of reliability in countless supply chains. As a result, significant opportunity exists for organizations willing to commit sufficient resources and energy to addressing these issues—more specifically, through implementation of digitalized solutions. For instance, real-time data can be leveraged to uncover supply chain problems faster while also forecasting future potential disruptions and issues.

THE CATALYST OF REMOTE WORK

The varied factors driving exponential change throughout industries and markets are reason enough to implement *Transformation* in your business. The proliferation of the remote work force absolutely mandates it.

An increasingly remote and dispersed workforce that lacks adequate digital security is little more than a security breach waiting to happen. Any business with a significant remote work force is only inviting disaster if it lacks sophisticated digital protection.

Breaking the situation down further offers additional evidence for the necessity of comprehensive digital protection. For one thing, while the implementation of platforms such as cloud service providers, data aggregators, and application programming interfaces that allow sensitive data to be shared with third parties is a necessary component of digital growth, it also opens up the entire system to a much greater cyber intrusion. In other words, the more people and places handling digital data, the greater the chance of a security break.

Another factor relates to the reality that several remote workers choose to do their jobs from their homes. While convenient and productive, it's also inherently less secure. From teenagers' school laptops to iPads, the connected devices within an in-home network that lack sufficient digital protection can offer a variety of tempting openings for criminals to exploit.

Addressing those issues and others begins with a remote digital work policy—something that many organizations may have to create from scratch. A solid policy should specify digital safety practices and procedures that all remote workers should follow. Setting standards, expectations, and processes for staff members is critical so that few, if any, questions regarding secure remote work habits go unanswered.

Begin with the devices used. Will employees use their own equipment or devices that the company provides? If employees have the option of using their own gear, what systems are in place that can test the safety and security of those devices?

Some workers, perhaps yearning for the greater socialization afforded by coffee shops and other similar settings, may ask if using unsecured public Wi-Fi is acceptable. Although it may offer greater flexibility, a broader network can be an open playing field for cybercriminals.

To further boost security, experts recommend that organizations require employees working remotely to use virtual private networks (VPNs) to help maintain complete data encryption. This effectively allows remote workers to send and receive information as securely as if their devices were connected directly to the organization's network.

Much of the challenge of maintaining digital integrity with a growing remote work force comes down to education. Offer comprehensive cybersecurity awareness training. Even though they're not on-site, remote workers should have the same level of access to technology support staff as their in-office colleagues. As part of their training, make sure they understand what issues or suspicious activities—such as phishing—warrant a call to a tech authority. Overreaction to, rather than disregard for, what might seem to be suspicious activity should be the ongoing rule.

Another challenge that might not seem directly related to security has to do with what may be called a remote work culture. Given the physical space between people working in an organization, how can a business replicate or devise a culture where remote workers feel the same cultural vibe at home that they do on-site? Therein lies the connection to security—if employees are focused on security in the office, that mindset should also be foremost away from the office, no matter where they happen to be doing their jobs.

But it goes beyond security. Even when working from home, employees should experience a sense of a professional environment. To that end, about 87 percent of companies believe building culture in remote teams is the foremost challenge in implementing an effective remote work system.[15]

One of the first epiphanies that many companies experience when implementing a significant remote work network is the impact of the absence of physical contact. No longer can an employee simply walk over to a colleague's desk to share a memo or chat about a particular project. Business automation software and other similar tools can help ensure such interaction over a physical divide is possible, allowing tasks and responsibilities to flow as smoothly as when everyone is in the same building.

The proper mindset can also contribute to a remote work attitude in line with the organization's culture. For instance, one major concern for any company considering or developing a remote work network can be labeled the "remote work excuse." Translated, it suggests that off-site employees fail to get their work done on time or up to established standards because they aren't in the actual office.

Approach that problem with the same commitment you would have to cybersecurity. Remote work should never be used as a reason for substandard performance. Additionally, it offers further evidence of the necessity of providing remote workers with every tool and system they need to maintain high standards. Employees should work to the highest levels of their abilities, no matter the setting.

Fostering a remote working culture—including an emphasis on digital security—should go beyond just asking your employees to work from home. First, evaluate your team's dynamics, then partner them with the right digital tools so that synergy and lasting relationships can be developed and maintained, no matter how far flung your workforce.

Understand and emphasize the reality of the situation moving forward. The workplace of the future will be digital and incorporate an off-site employee population. Be transparent and proactive about communicating this to everyone involved. Trust and commitment to that future vision will help ensure a digital workplace that is secure, dynamic, and inclusive.

DIGITALIZATION—A WEAPON AGAINST MISINFORMATION

Although a significant digital role can move your business into areas of innovation and productivity that more traditional business tools are incapable of reaching, one immutable truth remains about the nature of business itself.

Safety is an essential element of business in any setting. Few organizations or businesses can survive, let alone thrive, when conditions surrounding them are volatile or potentially dangerous—from natural disasters to military conflicts to political upheaval.

One critique about digitalization is that it effectively exposes businesses, organizations, and governments to a greater amount of vulnerability. As some would see it, the world is dangerous enough without adding an aspect that can be breached by some ill-intentioned hacker thousands of miles away. However off target, as prior sections of this chapter examine, it's nonetheless a pervasive fear, particularly among those who simply don't understand all aspects of a digital component.

But consider the issue from another angle. What if digitalization and all that it can encompass were used to predict, pinpoint, and expose hackers, misinformation, and other forms of online crime? In effect, how can a perceived weak point be used instead as a powerful weapon?

This is actually already happening, further substantiating the value of *Transformation* that also leverages digital technology.

One element of this is digital forensic science—a type of forensic science that focuses on the investigation and recovery of material related to cybercrime. Although the term *digital forensics* was first limited to computer forensics, it has since grown to cover the investigation of any devices that can store digital data. The ultimate objective is identifying, preserving, analyzing, and documenting digital data for use as evidence in a court of law, employing established forensic techniques to ensure the findings are admissible.

Another area that digitally based research addresses is fake news and other forms of misinformation. It's an understandably challenging undertaking. Among other issues, misinformation artists' ability to sculpt content with effectively deceptive window dressing can make identification difficult. Digital content with sophisticated graphics, quality photographs, intriguing headlines, and quality copy geared to attract attention can easily perform as well as, and often better than, legitimate news and information.

That leads to another hurdle. Well-designed fake news accomplishes its core mission—spreading to as many places and sources as quickly as possible. And, for better or worse, fast-moving content implies worth better than quality or legitimacy.

But digital tools can be employed to break through those barriers through comprehensive, ongoing assessment and analysis of representative samples of digital content. In effect, by compiling a library of emblematic digital content, digital technology can efficiently and effectively analyze material against what is considered to be "the norm"—including word phrasing, commonly used expressions, graphic accompaniments, and other elements.

It's not hard to picture such a system conducting widespread content sampling on an ongoing basis, pinpointing and analyzing both publishing and sharing activity. The system could monitor stories and news across a representative set of major websites, social media, and popular blogs. From there, it could build an exhaustive catalogue with which future content and where it moves can be compared. As a result, suspect content can be pinpointed if it extends beyond the bounds of what are considered reliable measures of legitimate material.

In addition, there's good news for those who fret about technology completely subsuming the role of human beings. A digital analytic system would be well served by a network of humans acting as autonomous reviewers who would not only monitor the output from any technical tool but also contribute their own observation and analysis. Additionally, the system could suggest particular elements for human reviewers to watch out for.

Coming together, that partnership could not only build a library of telling signs and signals but also examine news organizations, social media, and others' roles in the dissemination of fake material of all sorts. From there, reviewers could "vote" on what stories appear most credible to them and cite the reasons for their decisions.

ARTIFICIAL INTELLIGENCE—A FURTHER BOOST TO COMBAT MISINFORMATION

While technology and humans working together can unite in a potent effort to curb misinformation, artificial intelligence (AI) can move the effort into a completely different stratum.

For instance, in the example cited previously, where technology could direct human review to specific elements and content, AI-driven analysis could further the process by quantifying the reliability of both the story in question and any possible variants. Not only can this detect misinformation already in circulation, but social media entities can also be advised proactively about content that contains errors, concocted information, and misleading material before it is distributed. That allows social media to identify the likely trustworthiness of new content before it ever moves into the public domain, thereby either killing the material or alerting users about its sketchy content.

AI is also leveraged in other ways in the war against misinformation. For example, a particularly common source of disingenuous news and other similar material is fake social media accounts. Using a methodology called Deep Entity Classification, AI can spot fake accounts by analyzing their contact and interaction with other social media connections. As a result, in one telling example, Facebook took action against 1.7 billion accounts in the fourth quarter of 2021 alone.[16]

NATIONAL AND GLOBAL SECURITY— A CALL TO ACTION

Misinformation and hacking have by no means limited their victims to businesses and individuals. As is becoming more commonly known, entire nations, political organizations, and other public entities are also appealing targets. Most people don't need to be reminded about Russia's technical meddling in American elections, not to mention the cyberwar underscoring Russia's aggression against Ukraine. (It was no coincidence that Russia banned Facebook in the first week of its invasion of Ukraine, even though just a small percentage of the population actually uses the platform.)

The subsequent debate certainly cuts both ways. On the one hand, given technology's role in the spread of misinformation and other forms of tech-enabled "warfare," critics contend that spreading digitalization has contributed to political and economic instability.

An additional argument focuses on who has greater access to such tech tools. The same critics who worry about digitalization's capacity to foment instability also point out that resources such as digital technology are often more accessible to governments and individuals with ill intent. With enough financial means at their disposal, they're able to readily acquire what they want—those providing the technology, amply compensated as they are, don't concern themselves with how it will be used.

The argument has some validity. Again, common examples such as Russian hackers attempting to manipulate democratic processes powerfully illustrate what such technology can do in the wrong hands. As shown in a 2014 breach of the U.S. Office of Personnel and Management by China, foreign adversaries clearly view identity theft as a valuable national intelligence strategy. An Iranian attack on Wall Street and North Korea's hack of Sony Pictures further illustrate a consistent and diverse course of action described by some analysts as "death by a thousand hacks."

Such intrusions are increasingly taking place on a more individual level as well. An American's identity is stolen almost once every minute. According to the Federal Trade Commission, there was a 3,000 percent increase in cases of citizens' information used in fraudulent applications for government benefits in 2020 alone.[17]

Still another factor that makes digitalization a difficult security issue to address is those who build such technology. More and more, private companies develop products that impact fundamental rights. One such example is facial recognition systems—a legitimate privacy matter that has only recently come under some form of governmental regulation. Businesses and companies routinely mine personal data without permission—yet another common practice that government has been slow to counter.

This is a clear call to action to introduce more comprehensive control and legislation—not merely to rein in danger to individual privacy and safety but to combat digitalization's increasing threat to political and economic stability. This issue cannot be best addressed by countries acting exclusively on their own. Entities such as the United Nations, NATO, and other inclusive groups can address digital regulation and control as a central element of their overall missions.

Such groups could agree on regulations and standards for technology that are wholly consistent with core democratic principles. From there, individual countries could implement them in ways that best meet their individual needs and circumstances while remaining consistent with those of other nations.

Another issue is the simple matter of commonly accepted language. Currently, there is no clear definition that spells out when cyber aggression constitutes an act of war. This emboldens nations to aggressively pursue a program of cyber warfare since those targeted don't seem to recognize which acts warrant retribution—not to mention how to carry out any sort of punitive response.

One possible solution that's been suggested is the implementation of an independent tribunal empowered to investigate such attacks, perhaps similar to the Hague. Based on the tribunal's decision, leaders could then decide what sort of response is legally and ethically justified.

In the United States, government at all levels clearly needs to play catch-up in terms of ensuring protection and preservation of everything from national security to individual privacy. Protective infrastructure must be constantly strengthened and refined, particularly so that terrorist groups and adversarial nations such as North Korea are incapable of compromising national security through cyberattacks. Additionally, leaders need to develop—and share—a comprehensive playbook that lays out specific steps to be taken in response to significant cyberattacks.

The good news is that the United States can look to other countries that have already implemented cohesive cybersecurity measures. Some nations, such as Israel, have designated a single entity with the overall responsibility of defining and executing the country's cybersecurity agenda. This mandate includes the development of a cohesive national cybersecurity strategy consisting of more individualized programs, among them protecting the critical infrastructure of the country, mobilizing response to cyber incidents, defining cybersecurity standards, improving the cyber awareness of citizens, and strengthening cybersecurity capabilities throughout a variety of industries.

Domestically, progress is happening. More funding has been directed toward agencies such as the Cybersecurity and Infrastructure Security Agency and the General Services Administration's Technology Modernization Fund. In May 2021, President Joe Biden signed an executive order outlining new federal cybersecurity guidelines, including the creation of a cybersecurity safety review board for examining the aftermath of data breaches and cyberattacks, among other measures.

Additionally, the United States and other countries can look to partner more closely with the private sector through more consistent cooperation and information sharing. On March 1, 2022, the Senate unanimously passed the Strengthening American Cybersecurity Act of 2022. This measure requires critical infrastructure companies to report significant cyber incidents and all ransom payments to the Department of Homeland Security's Cybersecurity and Infrastructure Security Agency. President Biden subsequently signed the measure into law.

On the other side of the coin, tech leaders say the government can be far more aggressive in reciprocating, such as sharing reports of cybersecurity issues with companies that might be at risk. Since attackers routinely go after many companies with the same strategy, timely sharing of critical data could allow vulnerable companies to put protective measures into place proactively.

It seems reasonable to agree that digital technology is a double-edged sword, capable of both significant good and unscrupulous aggression. Countries throughout the world would do well to recognize this and to address both sides.

NEED TO KNOW:

- While many are concerned that a digital workplace is more vulnerable, research has established that digitalization can bolster security.
- Tasks as simple as sending material to a remote printer are now vulnerable to security breaches—digital's capacity for encryption can offset this.
- As more companies incorporate remote work into their organization, it's imperative that security measures are strengthened.
- Digitalization isn't limited to security issues. It can also be used to combat misinformation.
- Countries can no longer ignore or dismiss digital security. National security demands a comprehensive and cohesive digital policy.

CHAPTER 4

TRANSFORMATION: THE ADDED PUNCH OF ARTIFICIAL INTELLIGENCE AND MACHINE LEARNING

GOING DIGITAL IS WONDERFUL unto itself. But just opting for digitalization without the added impact of complementary technology is akin to getting electricity in the early twentieth century but choosing to never plug anything in.

Digital transformation, artificial intelligence (AI), and machine learning have become some of the most ubiquitous buzzwords in a world of technology that already has a lot to talk about. To that end, a variety of organizations are busy embracing these coupled technologies with the utmost enthusiasm. According to a report by International Data Corporation, worldwide spending on technologies and services that enable digital transformation is likely to reach $1.97 trillion by the end of 2022. Concomitantly, a Gartner CIO survey found that the implementation of AI has grown by a significant 270 percent over the span of a mere four years.[1]

Indeed, the players involved in such efforts have also changed significantly. Unlike two to three decades ago, when widespread technological innovation was pretty much the sole purview of technology professionals, today business leaders have also become involved in the effort. The overall focus has decidedly shifted to empower business management to access this technology to change and reinvent their entire organizations.

Once more, the accelerated adoption and use of digital technology alongside AI and machine learning can be attributed to a large extent to the COVID-19 pandemic. While it was a massive weight on the conduct of business as usual, the stagnation imposed by the pandemic also gave organizations an opportunity to sit back, think, recognize, and decide how to best leverage both digitalization and those accompanying powerful tools. A study by PricewaterhouseCoopers found that 52 percent of companies accelerated their AI adoption plans because of the COVID-19 crisis.[2]

And that short-term bump is not destined to end with the pandemic. Around 90 percent of companies refer to AI as a mainstream technology, with plans to further introduce and leverage AI's technological muscle. According to Gartner, one-third of technology providers with AI plans said they would invest $1 million or more over just two years' time.[3] Overall, corporate spending on big data and analytics is exploding, with European spending reaching $50 billion in U.S. currency in 2021.[4]

To those shrinking few who have yet to get a handle on what all the excitement and check writing is about, it can prove exceedingly helpful to see how AI and machine learning working in conjunction with digitalization can drive meaningful evolution and reinvention in most every business and organization. As is pointed out, going digital is certainly never an unwise option. Couple that with AI and machine learning, and any form of change becomes that much more transformative—and the resulting advantages and benefits warrant serious attention.

FUNDING ALLOCATED TO AI

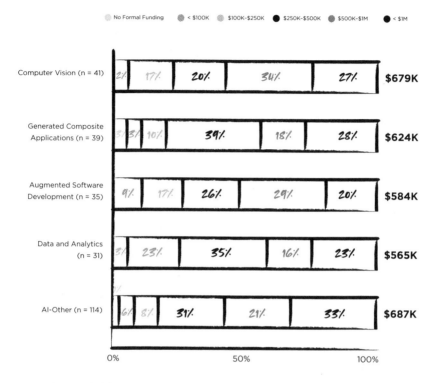

Legend: No Formal Funding · < $100K · $100K-$250K · $250K-$500K · $500K-$1M · < $1M

Computer Vision (n = 41): 2%, 17%, 20%, 34%, 27% — $679K

Generated Composite Applications (n = 39): 3%, 3%, 10%, 39%, 18%, 28% — $624K

Augmented Software Development (n = 35): 9%, 17%, 26%, 29%, 20% — $584K

Data and Analytics (n = 31): 3%, 23%, 35%, 16%, 23% — $565K

AI-Other (n = 114): 6%, 8%, 31%, 21%, 33% — $687K

0%   50%   100%

Figure 4.1. Level of funding allocated to AI emerging technologies.[5]

SOME BASICS—DEFINITIONS AND OVERALL BENEFITS

Unless you've spent the past few years chanting away in an isolated monastery—if you have, consider yourself lucky—or are so technology averse that you avoid the topics at every mention, it's hard to imagine anyone not at least having heard of AI and machine learning. Nonetheless, before tackling the varied potential and opportunity of digital transformation accompanied by AI and machine learning, it's prudent to offer a brief definition for those two terms:

The *Encyclopedia Britannica* offers up the following succinct definition:

Artificial intelligence (AI): the ability of a digital computer or computer-controlled robot to perform tasks commonly associated with intelligent beings. The term is frequently applied to the project of developing systems endowed with the intellectual processes characteristic of humans, such as the ability to reason, discover meaning, generalize, or learn from past experience.[6]

Seems simple enough. AI is a form of replication of many common mental capabilities. Moving forward with that just a bit, machines empowered with these "skills" can carry out tasks and responsibilities that were formerly exclusive to human beings. Let your imagination consider the possibilities of such a situation.

Now on to machine learning. Courtesy of the Massachusetts Institute of Technology, here's how that institution defines it:

Machine learning is a subfield of artificial intelligence, which is broadly defined as the capability of a machine to imitate intelligent human behavior. Artificial intelligence systems are used to perform complex tasks in a way that is similar to how humans solve problems . . . Machine learning takes the approach of letting computers learn to program themselves through experience.[7]

As a form of artificial intelligence, machine learning has the potential to allow the devices to learn as they go, so to speak.

So, how do companies and organizations stand to benefit? Unto themselves, combining the dynamics of digitalization, AI, and machine learning, the possibilities and opportunities can literally speak for themselves: Speed. Efficiency. Removal of tedious human tasks. Faster, more comprehensive research and analysis. All driven by a system that learns what to do pretty much by being turned loose and being allowed to learn.

Even from a 20,000-foot view, that's an appealing package. To get a more specific sense of potential benefits, let's examine just a few of them in greater detail. In one way or another, they'll all match up with one or more of the aforementioned functions and resulting metrics—core elements of any successful organizational *Transformation*.

GREATER REVENUE

To whet your appetite, let's begin with an appetizer that resonates with every profit-driven entity on the planet—revenue.

Simply put, the triumvirate of digital–AI–machine learning can drive significantly greater income for companies and organizations. As one bit of evidence, a survey-based report by Indian technology giant Infosys published in the *Enterprise* found that 98 percent of respondents who used AI-supported activities to power digital transformation had generated additional revenue—raising their bottom line by at least 15 percent.[8]

The reasons are both varied and compelling. In one respect, AI helps businesses bolster their digital transformation by increasing operational efficiency and mitigating risks while driving growth and innovation. Even to a rank layperson, that's not difficult to dissect. As the three components—digital, AI, and machine learning—make everything from routine tasks to sophisticated analysis faster and more efficient, so too are the expenses attached to such activities trimmed.

But financial import goes well beyond generalized lowered costs coupled with better outcomes. In fact, some might argue that AI has the greatest financial potential with regard to marketing, sales, and customer service. As for marketing, AI's capacity for detailed, expedient processing of varied data allows organizations to keep pace and better manage constantly increasing flows of information.

On a more specific level, AI establishes a reliable and efficient means of tracking buying decisions back to individual marketing efforts by channel. Not only does that, in effect, let management know what is working—success that can be quickly replicated in other areas, a boon to budgetary control—but also AI can locate specific points of opportunity, both in the timing of messages and to whom they are directed.

Closely related is AI's impact on sales. According to McKinsey research that appeared in the *Harvard Business Review*, sales teams that have adopted AI have increased leads and appointments by about 50 percent.[9] Additionally, as cited in the same study, machine learning lends a powerful assist by performing such time-draining tasks as connecting with leads, qualifying, and subsequent follow-up.

As for customer service, while this area is addressed in substantial detail later in this chapter, for now just think of an experience that is becoming increasingly common for all of us—the manifestation of AI in online and telephone chatbots. For its part, machine learning accentuates many of AI's benefits through greater customer personalization, allowing systems to better connect consumers with the optimal product or service for their individual needs.

Now to the very juicy bottom line. Reams of evidence and research confirm that digital transformation coupled with AI and machine learning can supercharge earnings. As data by Accenture cites, AI has the capacity to boost profitability in multiple industries by an average of 38 percent by 2035. In additional revenue alone, AI stands to power an extra $14 trillion.[10]

ANALYTICS

It's no earth-shaking epiphany that ample data and the tools with which to conduct a thorough study can greatly enhance decision-making. Up until recently, that was a matter of both time and sufficient people—the time with which to do the necessary work and enough people so that the entire process didn't drag out interminably.

Artificial intelligence and machine learning tackle both those requirements. Although a race pitting a human analyst against an AI-equipped device would be a ludicrous exercise, it's safe to say that AI's speed easily laps that of its two-legged counterpart. Moreover, the results are decidedly superior. For instance, a study by researchers at the University of California, San Francisco, trained a computer to assess the most common echocardiogram views and tested them against skilled human technicians. Using more than 180,000 real-world echo images, researchers determined not only that the machine performed markedly faster but that the computers also accurately assessed EKG videos 91.7– 97.8 percent of the time, compared to 70.2–83.5 percent when humans reviewed them.[11]

Taking that information outside a medical arena, AI and machine learning can transform both the quality and speed of access to all forms of critical business data. For example, lacking such capability, it would likely take some time for a retailer to follow up on an online customer's shopping interests. With AI and machine learning, that can happen as the customer is literally looking at the item that subsequently triggers the suggestion.

One step beyond this scenario is what some refer to as *dynamic analytics*. As I've already discussed, collecting useful data is essential to transforming the overall customer experience. But what matters perhaps even more is how that data is leveraged. AI processes thousands of data points to gather insights and identify trends in real time. This allows companies not only to react more quickly to consumers' actions but to effectively preempt the process with a recommendation that derives from real experience. From there, companies can quickly build personalized customer shopping experiences while also guiding any related marketing and public outreach efforts.

And all of this occurs in a fraction of the time that a human analyst would need to produce comparable results—if, at the risk of being glib, they're able to come up with anything even remotely as comprehensive.

It hasn't taken very long for companies and organizations of varied types to recognize the inherent potential. According to Dr. Marlene Wolfgruber, director of product marketing at ABBYY, 28 percent of organizations have identified the opportunity provided by AI and are planning to expand their process-mining and intelligence capabilities.[12]

Another positive element to the application of AI and machine learning is that it doesn't necessarily discount the contributions of living, breathing people. Referred to in one respect as *augmented analytics*, this is effectively a form of collaboration in which traditional human-produced reporting data and analytics are augmented by machine learning–derived data. Boiled down, the objective is to produce analytics that are easier to understand, more comprehensive, and produced from a greater range of sources. That helps ensure more thorough, reliable results.

The idea of augmented analytics has helped to address one area of concern regarding AI and machine learning—understanding just how a particular AI or machine learning device arrived at the conclusion or recommendation that it did. It's an essential objective and one that warrants serious attention moving forward—not merely because regulatory compliance mandates it, but, just as critical, so that companies and organizations are responsible for their decisions and actions based on the recommendations of AI and machine learning.

GREATER AUTOMATION

Although the capacity for AI and machine learning to automate a diverse range of processes and tasks is previously discussed in this book, the potential for automation on completely higher and more diverse levels warrants particular attention.

One element of AI and machine learning regarding automation is the sheer diversity of jobs and responsibilities that are now open to automation. In fact, automation can be broken down into three distinct subcategories:

- *Robotic process automation*: This is likely the form of automation with which most people are familiar—relatively simple, repetitive, routine tasks, such as delivery shipment tracking.

- *Cognitive automation*: This involves a step up from robotic-focused processes. Employing technology such as voice recognition or pattern analysis, this allows a device—such as a chatbot—to interact and, in a sense, interpret and respond to what it senses.

- *Social robotics*: Here, the technology functions a bit more autonomously while simultaneously interacting and working together with humans through the use of AI and devices such as sensors. See a driverless car pass by? That's social robotics at work.

In so many words, automation with the added muscle of AI and machine learning has moved well beyond the ability to carry out tasks and repetitive responsibilities that would bore any human being to sleep within seconds. Powered with AI, the applications of automation become much broader and, just as critical, more flexible. For example, if an unexpected event were to occur amid the work of more limited automated devices, the system would simply be unable to continue. On the other hand, if that device is capable of learning from and evaluating the situation, it can adjust to changing conditions and continue with its designated task.

Overall, the level of automation afforded by AI and machine learning stands to have a revolutionary impact across all sorts of industries. At its heart, this type of automation can target any number of work processes and responsibilities to bolster productivity, shorten the cycle time of everything from order fulfillment to the development and implementation of new products, and reduce any number of associated expenses.

One final word of comfort: As AI and machine learning proponents are quick to point out, the sort of automation afforded by these tools focuses on tasks and specific responsibilities—not jobs. However enormous the potential, the removal of the human element is not merely impossible but also unwanted. Collaboration, rather than replacement, is the ultimate formula and end goal.

GREATER CONSUMER ENGAGEMENT AND INSIGHT

The balance of power in the marketplace has undergone a tectonic shift in the past few decades. While producers of goods and services formerly held all the cards, so to speak—we make it, you buy it, end of narrative—consumers now levy far greater influence and control over what manufacturers produce, how they produce it, and how those consumers ultimately decide which to buy.

AI and machine learning allow businesses and organizations to take that new playing field head on—and they don't have to pore through customer feedback cards to do so.

Admittedly, a piece of cardboard that allows patrons to praise or complain is as outdated as spats and rumble seats. But also now outdated is the traditional analysis of customer interest and priorities that merely examined gauges such as traffic moving through a website.

Moreover, *Transformation* that's customer-centric and comprehensive is essential for business reinvention. The need for more agile, customer-focused approaches to overall transformation has never been greater. Analyzing and responding to customers' interests requires speed and flexibility not only to pinpoint consumer priorities of the moment but also to empower businesses to keep pace with consumers as their varied needs and wants evolve over time.

Digital transformation that incorporates AI and machine learning can empower such analysis by leaps and bounds. In one respect, AI can help optimize customer engagement by dynamically aligning the website content with the customer's preferences—recommending particular products, navigational hints, and other components that help build a more personalized and sensitive customer experience. Organizations that are the most successful with this aspect of digital transformation enjoy improvements in customer loyalty and satisfaction—and see those sorts of results faster than they might have ever hoped possible.

AI and machine learning also empower businesses with the capacity to track consumers' interests on a more proactive level. AI-based algorithms make it possible to create models based on customers' shopping and buying propensity. Leveraging predictive analytics, businesses can better gauge the probability of a given customer responding to a special offer, bundled special, email campaign, or other form of call to action. The benefits are extensive, including increased opportunity for upsell, cross-selling, more effective and focused marketing efforts, and overall greater customer retention and satisfaction.

The benefits are not limited only to those times when everything is going swimmingly. AI and machine learning also afford businesses the capacity to better and more efficiently address consumer issues, requests, and complaints. Technology such as conversational robotic process automation, which automates dialogue response and flow, can effectively address 65 percent of user requests and reduce the time needed to resolve issues by upwards of 90 percent—and, along the way, improve customer satisfaction scores by 80 percent.[13]

Once more, businesses and organizations are voting with their feet. According to one forecast by the analytic firm Gartner, by 2025, a large number of companies and organizations will supplement traditional surveys by using AI and machine learning in analyzing voice and text customer interaction.[14] The eventual outcome—an utter revolution in customer care and relationships.

SECURITY

Now it's time to address the proverbial elephant in the room.

As referenced earlier, digital naysayers often characterize technology such as digitalization as a veritable Pandora's box. Yes, it's undeniably valuable in many respects, but at the same time it carries a level of exposure that has made victims of countless entities and individuals. The greater the access to sensitive information, they argue, the greater the vulnerability.

One counter to that stance is the use of AI and machine learning specifically to address the issue of cybersecurity. Although security is rarely foremost among the priorities of any type of digital transformation, incorporating AI and machine learning can serve to boost the overall impact of reinvention—a *Transformation* that also reinvents an organization's cybersafety.

Some of the reasons AI can help in the digital safety wars are hardly surprising. For one thing, AI and machine learning continue to learn over the course of time. By ongoing recognition of patterns on networks and subsequent grouping according to common traits, they can detect any deviations or security incidents outside the norm. And, given the speed with which this all occurs, detection and appropriate responses can also occur that much faster.

Another plus is the capacity of AI and machine learning to identify unknown threats—a major cause of financial loss. Again, by constantly accumulating and analyzing behavioral patterns and trends, the technology is also able to pinpoint potential breaches that don't follow any sort of prior pattern. Further, AI affords a degree of automation to cybersecurity, such as systems checks and other forms of oversight to proactively identify potential problems.

Finally, AI and machine learning are security money savers. Greater efficiency, speed, and accuracy all come together to reduce the resources required to detect and respond to cyber threats—not to mention the sums of money saved by effectively spotting and combating cybercrime before it has a chance to inflict any meaningful damage.

By placing an emphasis on greatly strengthened security, organizations that leverage AI and machine learning in their safety measures are responding directly to a growing consumer priority. According to a recent Fraud and Security survey by Fiserv, a financial technology provider, 79 percent of consumers say that cybersecurity is equally or more concerning than it was for them a year prior.[15]

And, as forces mass and mature on both sides of the issue of cybersecurity, it's hard to imagine a time when digital safety will ever be taken for granted by a meaningful segment of consumers.

AI AND SUPPLY CHAIN ISSUES

Among other aftereffects of the COVID-19 pandemic, two things stand out that no longer take people by surprise:

- Someone wearing a protective mask in public—say, at the grocery store
- That same grocery store, once reliably stocked, now riddled with empty shelves

Groceries and other household supplies aren't the only items impacted by supply chain issues. From semiconductors to lumber, goods across the board have been in short supply due to disruptions caused by the pandemic crisis.

Once again, AI and machine learning stand at the ready to help begin the restocking process. For the most part, many companies and industries are still largely relying on manual means of managing their supply chains. But, as COVID-19 amply underscored, a manual system isn't ready to cope with widespread manufacturing lapses and subsequent failure to deliver those goods to dealers in a timely manner.

Analytics driven by AI can help companies predict, prepare, and react more quickly to supply chain disruptions. Through examination of patterns and forecasting of potential problems, AI can boost the speed and reliability of product transport and delivery. Speed, in particular, is one coveted benefit—45 percent of organizations cite faster speed to market as their primary goal in digitizing their supply chain with AI and machine learning–driven intelligence.[16]

Similar to other applications, AI promotes greater efficiency and use of human skills in supply chain management. As AI is capable of handling routine maintenance, minor problems, and other housekeeping measures, human intelligence is freed up to address more complex problems—with AI lending a helping hand through suggestions, strategies, or refinement of human-derived ideas.

AI AND SKILLS AND STAFF SHORTAGES

Do missing items at the corner market give you a headache? Imagine tackling those same shortfalls in trying to find qualified people for your business or organization.

The Great Resignation has hit industries across the board with staffing problems and skills shortages. Small wonder—when you have news reports citing millions who are voluntarily giving up their work for any number of reasons, empty cubicles and customer service desks can seem downright commonplace.

Among other countermeasures, AI is poised to address the situation in a variety of ways. In one respect, companies are boosting adoption of AI and similar tools to bolster the performance of remaining employees, many of whom may be dealing with additional workloads due to the labor exodus. Plus, AI can also strengthen companies' remote work network, making it more possible for workers to perform their jobs where they wish—one potential remedy to the mass dissatisfaction fueling the Great Resignation.

That dynamic can also be applied proactively. Through analysis of behavioral patterns, work quality, and other factors, AI could conceivably anticipate when an employee is nearing a point of handing in their two weeks' notice. Perhaps even more valuable, AI may offer insight into the reasons why an employee is interested in resigning. From there, management can take steps to head off a talented employee's departure or, at the very least, gather information that can be used to prevent other employees leaving in the future.

AI can also lend a hand with other issues driving worker resignation. For instance, mental health and burnout pose major issues, as people planning to leave their jobs commonly cite work stress as a major factor. AI-based solutions could help HR departments monitor employee satisfaction and provide more and better support to those who need it.

Additionally, AI can step up and effectively perform many functions that former human employees did—responding to calls, providing customer service, serving as cashiers, and assisting Human Resources in recruiting efforts, even on a *pinch-hit* basis as needed, should management later wish to restaff those positions with human employees.

Overall, AI and machine learning offer numerous valuable advantages to businesses looking to transform themselves. In fact, the pluses are multilayered—on one level, AI and machine learning unto themselves simply make the workplace or organization that much more productive and efficient, from streamlining processes to helping ensure that talented employees are as satisfied and engaged as possible.

On another level, AI and machine learning can further drive the over-all impact of any sort of *Transformation* that includes a significant digital component. In so many words, as the discussion in this chapter addresses, you and your organization stand to benefit more than you would if AI and machine learning were left out of the mix. And that can result in *Transformation* that simply doesn't go as far as it could or, worse, simply fails—a waste of time, energy, and resources.

NEED TO KNOW:

- Artificial intelligence (AI) and machine learning can broaden digital's capacity for transformation.
- AI can greatly boost a company's revenue streams through greater productivity and efficiency.
- AI and machine learning can perform comprehensive analytics far faster and more accurately than human beings.
- Automation through AI reduces boring repetitive work, freeing human employees for more challenging and rewarding tasks.
- AI and machine learning can also strengthen security while offering greater customer engagement and insight.

SECTION 2

SECTION 2

TRANSFORMATION VIA DIGITALIZATION— NECESSARY STEPS

THE CASE FOR TRANSFORMING your business or organization leveraging digital technology is undeniably compelling—so powerful, in fact, that even the briefest review of the advantages and opportunities seems needlessly redundant. What is anything but repetitive, however, is what it takes to get you where you want to go. Moreover, it isn't quite the checklist that many of us might expect.

True, you need an understanding of the essential technology involved (whether that will be you or some other tech-savvy individual). You need to know the optimal order in which things should take place. You should also have a clear set of benchmarks to track your progress and make certain that progress is occurring when and how it should.

But transforming your business involves a great deal more than unplugging this and plugging in that. It takes careful thought and a good deal of introspection. That's because *Transformation*, however focused on technical aspects, also involves a sweeping reinvention of a great deal—if not most—of your organization, including aspects that you may not expect.

That's just one of the many reasons why digital transformation falls short or outright fails. The overall scope of change can be simply enormous. Any company that fails to recognize that reality and plan accordingly is likely going to endure an effort characterized by struggle and missteps—or worse, complete disaster.

Fortunately, this fate is not cast in stone. There are countless entities that have reinvented themselves both completely and successfully—if it simply couldn't be done, there would be no such examples. But it stands to reason that, in those instances where transformation achieved its full potential, the overall effort was driven by careful preparation, thoughtful execution, and a candid transparency of the challenges of the task.

Let's make certain that describes your company as well—starting with a discussion of the varied challenges and obstacles that lie before you.

CHAPTER 5

RECOGNIZE THE CHALLENGES

EVERY PARTY NEEDS A pooper. And, with regard to *Transformation* with digital technology, there are apparently plenty of poopers to go around—starting with the more than eight out of ten planned *Transformations* that apparently fail.

According to Forbes, around 84 percent of digital transformations outright flop.[1] If you think that number is a gross outlier, other research also cites a frustratingly high level of struggles and missteps. According to an Everest Group study, 73 percent of companies failed to derive any business value from their digital transformation processes.[2] A Harvey Nash/KPMG CIO Survey pointed out that only 18 percent of companies rate their use of digital technology as "very effective."[3]

That's in no way meant to be discouraging. The benefits of digital transformation, however challenging the journey, are decidedly worth it. And, for the most part, leaders know that. A study by Gartner found that 87 percent of senior management in more than sixty companies labeled digitalization a company priority. Close to 80 percent said it's creating new revenue streams.[4]

So, it's clear that people recognize that digitalization makes complete sense. But what makes even more sense is pursuing digital transformation with your eyes wide open to the challenges and pitfalls you're likely to encounter—and learning how to skirt them as much as possible. As one company's makeup and priorities will differ from another, here—in no particular order—is a roster of common digital transformation roadblocks:

1. LACK OF COMMITMENT— STARTING AT THE TOP

Digital transformation is a sweeping, transformative undertaking. Lack of commitment among management can effectively sabotage the effort from the very beginning.

Leadership alignment and consistent commitment are critical to the success of digital transformation. Consider a scenario where certain members of management disagree or, at the very least, doubt the value of pursuing a digital reinvention. Not only can that prove problematic from the outset of the process, but lingering doubts and skepticism can also crop up at any later time, impeding progress at several different points. As I touch on later, that vibe can also drift down to others in an organization, effectively spreading doubt as well as confusion.

Accordingly, it's important to address issues of management commitment before even taking the very first step toward such a large initiative. One solid way is through a natural component of digitalization—the capacity to clearly quantify benefits. For instance, given that digital marketing and sales are easily measured, it's relatively simple to identify the return on investment of a digital program. Consider sending a test email using CSS media query, which segments browsers by certain characteristics, features, and user preferences. Compare its conversion rate with comparable results from other email campaigns, and you have an empirical, fact-based argument for digital transformation.

The more you can delineate benefits, the better the chances of gaining management buy-in—particularly from people who are not especially technology savvy. Positive results that can be documented are always compelling.

That segues into the value of understanding your audience. If you don't already know, take the time to identify what sort of case for digitalization others at the management level will most likely respond positively to. Again, ROI is always a solid bet, but others may prioritize different issues, such as greater work flexibility or the speed with which digital processes can deliver results. Building a case for digital transformation isn't a one-size-fits-all proposition—get to know those sweet spots that can best gain colleagues' support.

More importantly though, don't rush the process. Hitting the pause button to ensure that leadership is aligned before embarking on a digital journey is far more constructive in the long run, as opposed to jumping in and hoping that the skeptics simply come around.

2. LACK OF BUY-IN ELSEWHERE

OK, so you've got senior management on board with your planned digital transformation. That's a significant step, but it's just the first in working to ensure that your remaining colleagues and teammates are every bit as committed.

One common mistake made by leadership is undue emphasis on winning over top management while giving other parts of the company significantly less attention. Somewhat understandably, they believe that a gravity of sorts will somehow take care of the rest, inevitably moving down through the remainder of an organization and imbuing a solid sense of commitment as it goes.

That's a top-down dynamic, which, like many such assumptions, rarely plays out in actual practice. Digital transformation isn't something that leaders can mandate or do on their own, no matter how influential they might be in an organization. To use a sports analogy, a quarterback may have an absolute gun for an arm, but without a strong offensive line protecting him, receivers with reliable hands catching the ball, and a coaching staff mapping out plays that actually work, all you're likely to see are rocket passes that end up on the ground all over the field.

Admittedly, buy-in at the top is essential. But so too is similar buy-in throughout the remainder of the company. Management must leverage change agents and evangelists at various levels in an organization to push the pervasive level of commitment that's so essential to success.

The strategy isn't all that different from what works with high-level management. Offer empirical examples of how everyone through the organization will benefit from the sorts of projects that are career-movement catalysts—from greater efficiency and productivity to the opportunity to pursue more innovative and creative work.

Similar to management, know with whom you're speaking. Pinpoint those within an organization who will likely prove early adopters—the ones who "get it" before others might. If you get them on board, they may prove particularly effective—rather than listening to a leader preaching the word to the troops, people often respond better when they hear something from someone they consider more of a colleague.

However, as a leader, you can still do more to win over the rank and file. Digital transformation success requires management to be more than just philosophically aligned—doing little more than talking a good game. Instead, show your commitment through your actions, such as encouraging activities and goals that align with the *Transformation*. In a nod to transparency, share what you personally are doing as part of the overall transformative effort. People throughout a company who see a leader walking the walk will experience a legitimate form of commitment and may decide that there really is something remarkable and worthwhile to all that's going on.

Another strategy to encourage widespread buy-in is to identify salient benefits for employees and, from there, develop and implement a timeline in which those advantages begin appearing relatively early in the transformative process. For instance, by starting with a digital system designed to promote greater work efficiency, employees can see for themselves fairly soon how they stand to benefit from the overall effort. From there, they'll see the value of supporting a longer-range effort that propels those and other benefits.

3. LACK OF CLEAR OBJECTIVES

One common reason for an absence of commitment and comprehensive buy-in is a simple lack of clear objectives. However surprising that may seem, given the scope of digitalization, management often fails to clearly identify what it hopes to achieve. Instead, organizations often cite vague objectives, such as "greater financial savings," "more production," or, perhaps fuzziest of all, simply "going digital" because it seems the thing to do.

Those may be worthwhile goals, but they don't pinpoint where or how those objectives can be attained. They don't convey any specific value. Additionally, in terms of encouraging organizational support, those types of catchphrases aren't really sufficiently focused for people to understand how they might personally benefit. Self-interest is a powerful driver— something that may be difficult to see from an overblown phrase or description that really doesn't say anything.

To address this, apply the acronym-based SMART principle with regard to goals: **s**pecific, **m**easurable, **a**chievable, **r**elevant, and **t**ime-bound. Broken down a bit further, a more effective expression of objectives can include the following considerations:

- *Specific:* If you're hoping to achieve savings goals, where, precisely, would you like to see them occur?

- *Measurable*: What yardsticks are in place to measure savings? At what intervals can savings be measured?

- *Achievable*: Is the plan aggressive yet reasonable? For instance, an insurance company that dreams of cutting its underwriting costs in half within a year's time is experiencing just that—a dream. However, the goal of a 20 percent reduction achieved systematically over a five-year period not only is more reasonable but also engenders greater overall confidence.

- *Relevant*: Why do you want to save all this money? Will it be redirected back within the company to improve employees' work lives? Will the money be earmarked for greater shareholder dividends, increasing the company's investment appeal?

- *Time-Bound*: This doesn't just refer to how long the entire process will take, but also notes benchmarks along the timeline where significant progress can be marked—yet another form of encouragement for everyone to stay the course.

Obviously, savings is only one possible goal of *Transformation*. There are several other sample goals:

- A grocery store chain might aim to reduce its inventory restocking timeframe from six hours to four.

- Using digital design, a clothing manufacturer could look to trim product development lifecycle by 25 percent.

- A credit union may strive to migrate from a paper-based preapproval system to an online network, cutting the necessary review time to fewer than three minutes on average.

Another strategy that may prove effective involves working up what a colleague of mine refers to as a *premortem*. Backing up a bit, every company on earth is familiar with a postmortem, a recap of what went both right and wrong at the conclusion of a project. Conducting such an exercise prior to beginning the project—the proverbial premortem—allows organizations the opportunity to empirically speculate about various outcomes and benefits.

That offers multiple advantages. For one thing, by pinpointing a particular outcome, the organization has an opportunity to clarify, refine, and make it more specific—the sort of specificity effective goal setting requires. Additionally, running a premortem may identify possible benefits that have yet to be considered, such as opportunities for expansion into new markets. Lastly, a premortem also affords the chance to identify potential stumbling blocks and begin devising possible solutions before they actually occur.

4. FEAR OF TOO MUCH DISRUPTION

An appropriate amount of change is very much in the eye of the beholder. What seems like a sweeping, exciting form of *Transformation* to one person may terrorize another who can only foresee widespread disruption, uncontrolled activity, and even chaos.

This is a common failure point, particularly regarding commitment. A leader in a company may express verbal support for digital transformation and say that they can see the benefits. However, when it comes to doing what is necessary, and, in doing so, perhaps going outside of their comfort zone, that commitment may waver.

One initial effective step in dealing with this challenge employs wisdom that applies in most every area—complete transparency. Don't try to suggest to nervous types that disruption isn't likely to occur in an undertaking of such magnitude—rather, admit that disruption is *likely*. Even if there is disruption, that's a good thing, provided the disruption is for the better. Openly acknowledging this is not merely honest but may imbue skeptics with a bit more confidence—a lack of sugarcoating can mitigate some fears.

Additionally, and as part of your premortem, identify particular points and areas that might be disruption targets and, from there, plan proactively to address them. For instance, if the physical mechanics of *Transformation* will involve displacing people on a temporary basis, prepare them for remote work with the right tools and attitudes. Openly sharing such proactive plans with jittery skeptics can also alleviate some of their anxiety.

Although somewhat passive in nature, look at the disruptions that other companies have experienced: Are they similar to what you might expect, and, if so, how did they cope with them? Even outside examples can be compelling in convincing worried colleagues that others have run up against similar issues and overcome them.

Reinforce the positives. Again, some level of disruption is possible, but solid planning, flexibility, and execution can help temper a degree of disruption and ultimately place your organization in a much stronger position. Better financials, better working conditions, greater retention of top-tier talent: Aren't these worth a bit of disruption, particularly if there are plans in place to mitigate it as much as possible?

Finally, it's essential to help anxious colleagues understand that *Transformation* is no longer an attractive option but absolutely essential—it's critical to growth and even survival in a market where competitors across the spectrum are considering or have already embarked on such reinvention. For some, this may seem an unduly *in-your-face* approach, but, however blunt, that's the reality. However unnerving to some, it's an environment where the options boil down to two: transform or deteriorate. In other words, change or die.

Temper that by taking your time. Try to be empathetic by looking to understand that, in most cases, such concerns about disruption are inherently well intended. However, never forget that waiting too long can have negative consequences, including missed market opportunities and revenue loss from a delayed digital makeover.

5. MAKING IT ALL ABOUT THE TECHNOLOGY, NOT THE PEOPLE— INCLUDING YOUR CUSTOMERS

Tony Hsieh, CEO of Zappos, once noted that it's impossible to deliver great service with unhappy employees. That can prove particularly pertinent with regard to *Transformation* that incorporates digital reinvention.

Even those of us who are fairly distanced from technology can be drawn into the allure of it. All the shiny new equipment, not to mention the possibilities that it can engender, can make it very easy to get caught up in technology for technology's sake.

That can prove a destructive path to follow. Yes, all the new, cutting-edge tools can promise all sorts of wonderful possibilities, but, at the end of the day, it is the people impacted by all this technology who really matter—and they determine whether a *Transformation* is successful or even genuine at all.

That begins with the people within your organization. How will they be affected by all this change? Are you taking them into account when it comes to deciding the elements of the *Transformation* itself? Additionally, have you taken the time to ask them about the *Transformation*— what they would like to see in it, and what they would like to derive from all that reinvention?

That makes communication and transparency essential. Don't merely convey what you see as the possibilities of *Transformation*—let them offer their input as well. You might be pleasantly surprised by suggestions that never occurred to you.

Communication about the impact of *Transformation* on those with whom you work can also greatly strengthen commitment and buy-in. If your people believe they're genuinely being considered—that their opinions truly matter—they'll be that much more invested in the success of the project.

But don't just stop there. Don't overlook the impact on your clients and customers as well. As noted previously, consumers are assuming an ever greater and more influential role in the marketplace. Their needs and desires are evolving. They're not the least bit shy about flexing their muscles. Certain products and features are blossoming from *like-to-haves* into rock solid expectations.

Don't assume you know what customers want in terms of technology, service, and other elements. Take the time to do some comprehensive market research. Get a clear picture of what they want and how they want it delivered, and, from there, take those into account when crafting your digital transformation.

6. IGNORING THE REALITY OF CULTURE CHANGE

Overlooking the impact of transformative change on people ties into another form of destructive tunnel vision—failing to see that digital transformation means culture change as well.

Don't make the mistake of assuming, as many organizations do, that once there's new technology in place, the entire *Transformation* is complete. Not by a long shot. In a very real sense, digital transformation has relatively little to do with the technology itself. Rather, it's about the organization itself—how adaptive it is, how comfortable it is with flexibility, and how ready it is to dump habits and mindsets of the past in favor of adopting new, more applicable considerations. Lacking those attributes, all the shiny new equipment in the world will, at best, function at the very minimal of its potential.

Digital transformation success relies on the right kind of culture. Leadership, planning, thoughtful execution, and a commitment to a fresh mindset are every bit as critical to success as the right technology. Consider the following questions:

- Would you characterize your company as forward thinking or more focused on the past?

- Does your company do things because they've always been done that way?

- Is cross-communication between departments encouraged or ignored?

- Is your company reasonably comfortable with risk, or does it avoid it whenever possible?

- Does your organization welcome input from as many as possible or adhere more to the proverbial party line?

- Would you describe your company as adaptable or flexible?

By now, you can see where these and other similar questions are headed. To implement a genuinely effective *Transformation* that includes a digital element, a welcoming culture must be in place, not merely to absorb the change but to drive it forward as well.

Many of the issues this chapter touches on can help with building the right culture. Establishing solid commitment and buy-in through the organization, adhering to transparency, and continually focusing on the impact upon people can all contribute to a culture that's open and welcoming to extensive change. Moreover, living your values, rather than just talking about them, can also foster a similar attitude in those around you, which are all part of an effective, coordinated effort.

Take steps to encourage a more horizontal, cross-departmental form of synergy. A siloed arrangement where people largely work autonomously naturally limits creative and innovative synergy. Additionally, work to build a greater comfort level with risk-taking. Implementation of a digital environment is inherently going to involve some trial and error—once people are more at ease with that, carry that mindset forward. Be comfortable with failure, fail fast, learn from the experience, and move on.

Make certain to provide adequate training and education. There are bound to be elements of your organization's reinvention that, from a digital standpoint, people aren't accustomed to or even familiar with. Training with the goal of making people not only technically capable but also able to apply those new skills with a completely different mindset fosters commitment, employee retention, and the habit of looking at things in a very different light.

Lastly, bear in mind that the journey never really ends as such—*Transformation* is never just *one and done*. Adjust your attitude to this more malleable mindset, and you'll skirt the mistake that everything's finished, and you can just sit back and relax while your competitors, who recognize a much longer timeframe, are busy adding distance between themselves and you.

7. LEGACY, TECHNOLOGY, AND PEOPLE

Mistaking mere replacement or updates for out-and-out transformative technology is yet another stumbling block for effective reinvention.

Beginning digital transformation with a large, costly legacy-replacement project is merely the starting line to running the wrong race. For one thing, replacing outdated systems with newer versions of the same thing can be exceedingly expensive. The same goes for updates—it's like trading in a leather buggy whip for one made of modern materials. It's expensive, energy sapping, and, perhaps most importantly, incapable of offering the lasting, meaningful change that genuine digital transformation does.

The same goes for the people involved in the *Transformation* itself. Don't assume that everyone currently under your roof will be all you need to reach your digitalization goals. It's imperative to work with people who specialize in digital transformation. If need be, look outside of your company for the right personnel to help. Additionally, the benefits may not be exclusively immediate and short lived. By establishing a relationship with a team with proven digital chops, you're also setting up a go-to source for guidance and advice moving forward.

8. INADEQUATE FLEXIBILITY

Given the exponentially increasing speed with which technology, the marketplace, consumers, and the workforce are changing, organizations that lack the inherent capacity to quickly adjust planning and execution may fail to overcome shifting challenges and conditions. *Transformation* incorporating digital technology is a long, winding road with no one definitive itinerary. What may work beautifully with one organization may be utterly inappropriate for another.

Digital transformation takes many strategies, tactics, and experiments—the hallmarks of a flexible organization. The capacity to be reasonably comfortable with failure and missteps and, from there, to keep moving forward mandates an organization at ease with pivoting on the fly.

Those characteristics are essential to *Transformation* that includes a digital element. For one thing, despite all the attention paid to digitalization, it's still a relatively new phenomenon. Although a rapidly increasing number of companies are turning to digital, there isn't necessarily an extensive and established playbook that everyone follows—in fact, far from it.

That makes flexibility critical. Odds are reasonable that one organization will encounter any number of completely unexpected challenges and obstacles that other companies are wholly immune to. Reacting quickly and confidently is important to deal with issues as they appear.

The speed with which digitalization takes hold also mandates flexibility. The faster things come at you, the faster you need to adapt and respond. Moreover, that rate of speed is only increasing, making flexibility particularly valuable moving forward.

One good starting point at which to develop or strengthen your organization's flexibility is to constantly examine and refine your business model. It's critical to continually revise, streamline, and, if need be, expand your existing business model in response to changes in your industry, customer base, and other factors.

Collaboration is also an essential component of flexibility. Rather than stratified work models that keep employees and teams in their proverbial lanes, encourage cross-collaboration and synergy. Solutions can often come from the unlikeliest of pairings.

An organization with flexibility also places an exclusive premium on results, rather than processes. Akin to cross-collaboration, a flexible company doesn't concern itself with how solutions happen, but rather that a viable solution is found. The destination matters, not the journey itself.

To that end, one defining characteristic of a flexible organization is a commitment to absolute transparency and ongoing communication. That's particularly true during periods of drastic transformation and change, where people can be understandably anxious about the impact of change on their futures. Keep people in the loop as much as possible to keep momentum going and eliminate any possible misunderstandings.

Obviously, there are many more potential challenges an organization may encounter during a digital transformation, but no matter the issues, knowing that they're likely to appear and preparing your organization with a capacity to respond adaptively are essential to ensuring that no single challenge is a deal killer.

Regardless of how your company readies itself for *Transformation*, much of the success or failure of the eventual outcome will focus on leadership—how those leading the charge perform in a disruptive, shifting environment. The mechanics of their leadership, their style and capacity to encourage commitment and innovative thought, and their ability for fast, flexible decision-making will be challenged throughout the entire process.

In short, leadership is everything—the exclusive focus of the next chapter.

NEED TO KNOW:

- It's essential to gain commitment and buy-in throughout an organization—from management to everyone impacted by *Transformation*.
- Make certain your goals for *Transformation* are clear, specific, and highlight how all members of the company may benefit.
- Expect some within your organization to be uncomfortable with disruptive change. Continue to emphasize the positive outcomes that a successful *Transformation* will foster.
- Don't get caught up in the technology. The impacts of *Transformation* on your people and culture are just as important.

CHAPTER 6

LEADERSHIP IS EVERYTHING

USING THE LEADERSHIP SKILLS, habits, and strategies of the past to provide effective guidance amid the flux of digital transformation is like a modern army commander mapping maneuvers for a horse-mounted cavalry: There's no connection—orders are going out to something that just doesn't exist anymore. It's completely irrelevant—what does exist will find any orders it receives confusing or utterly intelligible. It simply won't work—no matter the specifics, the eventual outcome will be, at its best, slipshod and scattered, and at its worst, outright disaster.

That argument slips nicely into the real world as well. Taking a brief step back, today's conventional interpretation of leadership was developed to address the challenges of the Industrial Revolution more than 200 years ago. There was no discussion of employee well-being, no interaction with customers about new products or services, and little or no attention paid to how the public viewed business ethics. Rather, it was pure hierarchy—as things needed to be done, orders were handed down and followed. Simple and authoritarian. An eighteenth-century version of "just do it."

That approach is utterly ill-suited to the modern workplace, let alone a workplace in *Transformation* involving digital tools and resources. One reason is, akin to the analogy at the start of this chapter, the recipient of such direction essentially doesn't exist—or at least is no longer completely intact. Factory work floors and construction gangs have been largely replaced and augmented by an array of individual specialized departments, technology that evolves by the minute, and a workforce that is increasingly off-site.

But those changes, however significant, pale when compared to the potential consequences. Old models of leadership relied on the assumption that workers were not worthy of trust and, as such, would only perform purely out of self-benefit. Additionally, bygone styles of leadership planned according to the amount of data available—limited information meant limited and inflexible long-range planning.

Imagine putting those two elements—leadership founded on suspicion and planning constrained by minimal information—into a work setting composed of a different sort of employee and built around technology that's evolving increasingly faster. That's a dangerous fuse waiting to be lit. It's complete disconnection.

That's why, even though the issue of leadership is addressed throughout this narrative, it decidedly warrants a chapter of its own. When it comes to leadership in an era characterized by flux, the stakes are simply that much greater.

Being an effective leader during and after digital transformation mandates more than a few tweaks and updates. Rather, it calls for a completely new way of thinking and acting derived from an appreciation of the magnitude of change taking place, as well as a new way of communicating with others involved in that effort.

Digital transformation can flourish or flounder based on a leader's ability to move away from a focus on management and toward one of leadership. It's imperative to offer vision and support through different avenues, rather than merely handing down directives. In doing so, a leader can drive disruption, help that disruption achieve all that it can, and instill a similar sense of possibilities with colleagues, teammates, and everyone else within an organization.

That's more than enough to earmark a detailed examination of leadership in a digital world.

TRULY UNDERSTAND WHAT'S GOING ON

For anyone with experience in leadership, the heading of this section may seem like a strange admonition. However, when it has to do with *Transformation* with a digital component, it's a perfectly valid issue to raise.

Many leaders fail to understand what it is they're trying to do with digital transformation—starting with an understanding of relevant terminology. Various studies have suggested that only a small fraction of executives grasp what is necessary to achieve *Transformation* that's consistent with shifts in their industry and markets.

That's not entirely their fault. As technologies of all kinds evolve and transform at an exponentially faster pace, keeping up with clear and relevant definitions of just what's what can seem a fool's errand.

But it's not. However challenging, it's critical that everyone within an organization—leadership and others—have a solid grasp of what certain tools and practices literally involve. And that can start with grasping the significant difference between three terms relating to digital transformation—*digitization, digitalization,* and *digital transformation* itself.

That isn't merely an issue of familiarization. Those three terms embody differences that truly matter. Depending on which particular option you pursue, each one will have different implementation paths, final outcomes, and related benefits and caveats.

In a sense, the three terms represent something of a logical and more comprehensive progression, each marking a particular point of maturation, although, as is noted later, it's not necessarily a matter of having one element of digital technology in place before proceeding to the next.

Let's start with digitization.

Digitization

The most limited of the three, digitization is the process of converting information contained in physical documents from analog to digital. In so doing, digitization involves taking information and encoding it so that it can be processed, stored, and transmitted electronically.

A variety of known examples of digitization exist. In a somewhat global, generic instance, digitization takes handwritten or typed text and moves it into a digital format. Another example that many people are familiar with is transferring bank statements from a paper-based format into computer-accessible material. A third case involves the electronic storage and distribution of health-care patients' records in lieu of more traditional paper-filled folders.

Digitization isn't limited only to business matters. You've probably signed a legal document online using an electronic format. You've also likely taken old VHS tapes with content you value and moved them into a digital format such as a DVD—another version of digitization.

The benefits of digitization are fairly apparent. In a business setting, storing records electronically not only can make them easier to manage and distribute as needed but also lends a higher degree of security. Additionally, digitization can make an entire operation more efficient by reducing the time and expense it takes to handle material in more traditional paper-based forms.

Digitalization

Digitalization is next on the list. In a nutshell, this involves leveraging technology to transform existing business models, thereby allowing organizations to use data in a more meaningful and comprehensive manner. In other words, it's a step up from digitization.

The increased importance of digitalization in business is more prevalent and readily apparent today than ever before. One very visible example is the application of cloud computing to store and distribute all types of materials. Another is the creation of automated workflows, such as order fulfillment. Breaking this down a bit further, a customer on a business's website places an order, a shipping label is automatically created, the item is subsequently prepared for shipment, and the customer is invoiced for the purchase—all automated without the need for a single manual task. That, in turn, generates lower operating costs and produces greater revenue.

But digitalization goes further than merely making things move faster and more efficiently. Addressing an area of exploding value and importance, digitalization can also gather and analyze critical customer data, such as product history and other meaningful trends. As a result, a business can not only gain greater insight into a customer's prior habits and preferences—a boon to cross-selling products and services—but also apply such analysis to the development and introduction of products and activities that are likely to be well received in the market. In that regard, digitalization can effectively involve the customer in what a business chooses to pursue.

Digitalization can also help in boosting a business's persona. A large portion of consumers today are experienced digital users who are so well-versed that they come to expect a similar level of maturity from the companies with which they choose to do business. Consequently, companies with a sophisticated digital presence—represented by an appealing and efficient website, for example—can better connect with the growing number of consumers who value that.

Digital Transformation

Digital transformation marks the last and most meaningful step in the digital journey. It's all about changing the way you run your business by reorienting existing processes within a new digital avenue. It's revisiting and reinventing everything that takes place, from internal systems to customer interaction (not to mention culture). By fully understanding the genuine potential of technology, you can use it as the catalyst to totally transform how your business operates—to make it into a digital business from top to bottom.

Examples of the benefits of digital transformation abound. In marketing, digital transformation allows businesses to up their games by connecting more thoroughly with prospective customers, as well as longtime loyalists. Digital marketing makes analytics tracking and subsequent dialogue with customers more comprehensive and efficient at the same time.

Those benefits carry over to sales. The capacity to collect large amounts of precise data on consumer behavior allows sales teams to approach consumers as individuals with defined likes, dislikes, and overall preferences. That lets them develop deeper bonds with customers, from initial contact through to the actual purchase point. Additionally, digital transformation inherently makes organizations more flexible and better able to adapt and respond to shifting customer values and activity.

Digital transformation also carries enormous internal benefits. For one thing, digital transformation is naturally complementary to a workforce that is increasingly remote. Flexibility is a major point of appeal to remote-friendly employees, and digital transformation boosts the ability to work from anywhere by automating a variety of processes, from analytics and reporting to complete project management.

Digital transformation can also address the traditional distrust of security when it comes to a remote workforce. Via digital transformation, companies can offer tools that automatically flag suspicious emails, add multifactor authentication and encryption to any device, and keep all confidential information exclusively accessible via virtual private networks.

Many manufacturing companies pursuing digital transformation are doing so in hopes of achieving greater overall efficiency. Digital transformation can improve manufacturing by employing predictive analytics to reduce supply chain costs, maintenance requirements, and consumption of energy and water.

The impact and benefits of digital transformation are also evident in financial services. On top of mobile banking and cash apps, consumers now use cash airdrops, cardless payments through services such as Apple Pay on phones or watches, and completely *bankless banking*—digital transformation that impacts nearly every element of the banking experience.

Although digitization–digitalization–digital transformation may seem like a one-step-to-the-next progression—and in terms of capability, it somewhat is—digital transformation doesn't necessarily involve a linear pattern. For instance, a company may implement one or more individual digitalization projects, from automating processes to training employees to using new technology and tools.

On the other hand, digital transformation isn't something that organizations can build by way of stand-alone initiatives. Instead, digital transformation encompasses almost every element of a business. That calls upon an entire organization to deal better with change overall, essentially reconstructing every aspect of core competency, as well as the culture built around the new technological framework. And all that can't happen in a piecemeal manner.

That, as is addressed earlier and in detail in subsequent portions of this book, has a great deal to do with companies' relationships with their customers. Customer muscle and influence in how organizations function are growing with every single minute. More organizations are becoming customer-driven from one end to the other. Digital transformation allows businesses to embrace this reality and leverage it through an accompanying transformation of their very culture.

Leadership needs to know this form of change intimately and, as a result, change the elements of their leadership as well.

DEVELOPING A DIGITAL MINDSET

No matter the preeminent objective, leaders are ultimately charged with fostering a mindset that effectively supports whatever initiative, project, or effort may be involved. That effort to build buy-in is particularly critical when it comes to digital transformation.

As noted by Abbey Lewis of Harvard Business Publishing in the *Harvard Business Review*, a digital mindset actually has very little to do with becoming fully versed in all aspects of digital technology: "Rather, it means having a foundational awareness of digital technology and the possibilities it opens up, and the willingness and ability to pursue new opportunities based on that awareness."[1]

In other words, a digital mindset starts with a certain comfort level with—and knowledge of—digital technology and, from there, leveraging them to confidently use digital technology to address situations and solve problems. A digital mindset is far more about attitude than it is acquired skill and ability. It lends attention to the growth possibilities available through digital transformation and a willingness to experiment—and even fail. It also approaches the adaptation of digital tools as a learning opportunity, rather than some form of must-pass examination.

Not surprisingly, developing a digital mindset starts at the very top of any organization. First, as they say, walk the walk yourself. It's essential that leadership be the very face of digital transformation. Support for digital transformation must be genuine, actionable, and visible, not to mention *inclusive*. Communicate consistently with all involved about the importance and value of digital transformation. Spearhead and boost relevant projects and other activities that not only move *Transformation* forward but boost overall support at the same time.

With regard to the various objectives involved in digital transformation, it's essential not only to be crystal clear about varied goals and the rationale behind them but also to keep the rest of the organization engaged and in the loop as much as possible. It's crucial to get everyone speaking the same language. With reference to a central issue cited earlier in this chapter, make certain that key terms and definitions are easy to understand. Avoid the use of jargon that many individuals and departments may use but that may be unfamiliar or baffling to everyone else. If you have technically savvy employees who are eager to adopt a digital environment, be sure to encourage them to bring others on board and to use language that everyone can grasp.

As part of fostering a digital mindset that supports digital transformation success, work to develop an environment where it's acceptable to mess up, if only on occasion. This is admittedly one of the foremost leadership challenges related to digital transformation, as many organizations are unfortunately steeped in an environment where mistakes and missteps are construed as incompetence and not tolerated. Instead, encourage thinking and ideas that run counter to the conventional and traditional—along with the confidence that failure is merely part of a journey that leads to greater things.

Be as candid as possible about your technical expertise—or, if more truthful, lack thereof. It may well be the case that your leadership position doesn't derive from your technological know-how—at least up to this point. If that's the case, let others know that you're going to be learning and growing as much as they are. Consistent with a commitment to transparency—and a comfort level with making mistakes—leaders who are open about their tech skills not only engender trust but also bolster a sense of collaboration by inviting others to help them along their journeys to develop greater tech chops.

AN EMPHASIS ON
GREATER COLLABORATION

The degree of change brought on by digital transformation can tempt some leaders to turn back to a more autocratic form of leadership that translates into something like the following: The change we are going to experience is dramatic. It's not in our best interest to leave this open for discussion. Therefore, I hand down orders—you follow them. Repeat.

However enticing, that is decidedly not the sort of leadership to pursue amid sweeping change. If nothing else, by the time you've moved to the last step, the only thing that may be repeating is the sound of doors closing as dissatisfied employees dash for a more democratic setting. Digital transformation can be unnerving enough—the addition of a dictatorial leadership style (also known as an old-school "transactional" leadership model, which is discussed in my previous book, *LIFT*) can not only sharpen anxiety but also push people out of the organization that much faster.

Accordingly, when beginning a journey of *Transformation* as comprehensive as one that includes a digital element, it's wise to adopt a more collaborative form of leadership as well as greater collaboration throughout the entire organization.

Let's begin with a clear definition of collaborative leadership. Collaborative leadership involves managing people in a way that crosses practical and organizational lines. The key word in that prior sentence is *manage*, not control. Collaborative leaders utilize influence rather than the authority of their positions to encourage, align, and inspire people to perform at their very best.

Collaborative leadership is further characterized by other practices and mindsets:

- The free dissemination of information, taking in all aspects of the organization

- Cross-functional and interdisciplinary teamwork

- Encouragement of employees to contribute through feedback and input, thereby boosting a sense of ownership

- A greater emphasis on arriving at decisions as a team

Taken together, the argument for collaborative leadership makes a compelling case. First, once again, never take for granted the degree of disruption and uncertainty that can infest any form of transformation. If nothing else, with collaborative leadership encouraging a sense of "We're all in this together," anxiety about the ultimate outcome of *Transformation* can be minimized.

Taking that issue a step further, a well-documented stumbling block to effective *Transformation* is needless siloing—autonomous departments and people working with little cooperation or collaboration. In one respect, that's an obvious route to problems—with the shared challenges of digital transformation, people consciously working apart from one another can only make what can prove to be an uphill climb even steeper.

Moreover, it seems to be a pervasive problem. In one study by Accenture, 75 percent of the 1,500 senior executives surveyed said their different business functions were competing rather than collaborating on digitization.[2]

That cuts at the very heart of digital reinvention. Moving an organization into a digital environment naturally promotes greater collaboration—in many ways, that's what digital transformation is all about. Further, collaboration isn't really a choice when it comes to digital transformation—new technologies are quickly reshaping roles and requiring collaboration between teams who might have never worked together before.

Lack of collaboration can also make digital transformation needlessly redundant—investing in digital technology in varied areas unnecessarily—and more expensive. In the Accenture study cited earlier, executives surveyed expected a 6.3 percent increase in costs as a result of avoidable, unnecessary spending.[3]

Collaborative leadership during digital transition and thereafter can address these and many other issues that consistently hamper many types of digital transformation. Not surprisingly, there are various ways to develop and nurture collaborative leadership. Following are a few suggestions worth pursuing:

1. Encourage a sense of shared purpose. A powerful feeling of common goals can naturally boost teamwork. For instance, during digital transformation and thereafter, look to projects that naturally bring people together—particularly if those people had little or no prior contact.

2. Empower people. Give colleagues and teammates genuine authority. This can boost the speed at which results take place while also strengthening trust.

3. Encourage innovation. Creativity and flexibility can be powerful tools in an unfamiliar environment.

4. Encourage feedback. The people doing the work itself know it better than anyone else. If they have something to share, take the time to listen.

5. Be as transparent as possible when it comes to decision-making. Knowing the why behind a particular choice is inclusive.

A digitally transformed work environment cannot take hold and grow within a stratified setting. Collaborative leadership is completely consistent with digital transformation—both during the process itself and in the work environment that results.

YOUR CULTURE IS CHANGING— MAKE CERTAIN IT'S SUSTAINABLE

As has been addressed before, transforming your business digitally also carries a meaningful culture change—by necessity. Any work setting whose culture doesn't evolve toward one characterized by collaboration, flexibility, and comfort with experimentation and occasional failure won't be in sync with a digital environment. By definition, a digital work setting absolutely mandates those attributes. Plus, a beneficial shift in culture should also be sustainable.

Allowing people and processes to slip back—often unconsciously— into old habits of work and mindsets can undo what would seem to be a successful reinvention. Accordingly, communicate with staff and others often, reminding them to check themselves for signs of slippage—for example, lack of collaboration, inadequate communication, or hesitancy to experiment.

From there, encourage employees to express sustainability in what they do. A culture with solid, long-term prospects is characterized by everyone proactively thinking about how sustainable practices can be implemented in their teams and departments. What seems to be consistently effective in what they do? If there is little to no sign of this, what can be tweaked to bolster sustainability? After all, these are the people on the front lines— they know better than anyone what's going to stick versus what's likely to become outdated. And, again, make certain people feel safe about expressing their ideas, however blunt or potentially controversial.

Another hallmark of a sustainable digital mindset and culture is an ongoing focus on growth and the potential of *tomorrow*. One effective means to address this is to proactively encourage staff and employees to submit ideas to promote innovation and growth—another aspect of the value of collaboration and a comfortable, welcoming, supportive environment.

Be sure to track progress of the implementation of a long-lasting culture change. Pursuit of long-term sustainability is greatly strengthened by employing key performance indicators (KPIs) that offer empirical measurement of progress. With access to clear KPIs, employees have a better understanding of not only what is, in fact, changing for the better but also how they can contribute to further that progress. Positive numbers are motivational.

Finally, don't feel as though the success or failure of *Transformation* is your sole responsibility. Work to make everyone accountable for building a healthy culture that endures. While leadership may be charged with mapping out strategy, others within an organization must also recognize a stake in the outcome—their own personal responsibility for their hand in what eventually takes place. Empowerment, collaboration, and commitment to constructive feedback will help ensure a culture whose longevity and benefits reflect the many hands who helped build it.

EMPHASIZE ETHICS

Of course, nothing is perfect . . .

Amid all the excitement and possibility that can define digital transformation is a particular caveat—the discomfort and varied misgivings many people have about both documented and potential abuses and excesses of rapidly evolving technology.

Let's start with the issue of data privacy. According to one study by Deloitte, close to 90 percent of people taking part in the research labeled data security a "very critical" issue that needed to be addressed over the next several years.[4] That concern is certainly understandable, given multiple instances in which enormous databases have been breached over the past number of years. As an example, in what's often considered the largest data hack in history, in 2016 Yahoo revealed a data breach that compromised more than 1 billion accounts.[5]

(As if that wasn't troubling enough, Yahoo's disclosure came around three years after the actual breach—not exactly the sort of upfront transparency that many jittery users would like to see.)

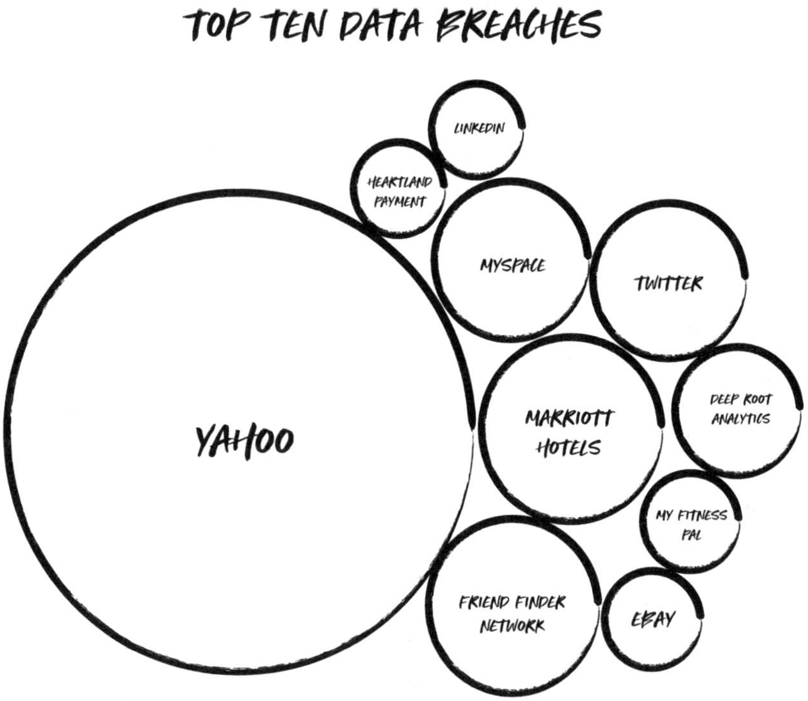

TOP TEN DATA BREACHES

Figure 6.1. Ten largest data breaches.[6]

Adding artificial intelligence to the mix only seems to make anxiety escalate. From its application in everything from health-care decisions to driverless cars, many are worried about AI's adherence to fairness, reliability, and the capacity to explain in understandable terms how it comes to make the choices that it does. For many, inherent bias in AI only makes the technology more suspect.

There are other concerns as well. As digital technology grows in its use, application, and impact, those features are as available to those with questionable motives as they are to the most legitimate company or organization, which may result in misinformation. Environmental sustainability is also in question. Just how will a growing digital presence impact efforts to combat climate change, global warming, and other issues? To cite just one point, how much energy will all this extra digital *oomph* require? And from what sources?

It seems that a gauntlet has been thrown down between digital presence and ethical behavior. On one hand, the enthusiasm that many organizations might have for the enormous opportunity inherent in digital transformation is utterly justifiable. On the other, critics have valid points. For example, numerous data breaches have occurred in the past. If digital transformation continues to proliferate, will that mean a concomitant jump in privacy and security breaches?

Observant companies will interpret the situation as a clear call to action. Accordingly, they'll also recognize the necessity of taking steps to ensure that any *Transformation* with a digital aspect also includes proactive policies, procedures, and other measures to ensure digital security and ethics as much as possible—now and in the future.

One solid initial step is to integrate ethics into company strategy from the very beginning. Establishing an ethics board or designating a chief ethics officer can prove valuable not merely in the transformative stage but thereafter as well. A board or individual whose sole purview is ethical strategy and execution can work closely with various departments and people to help steer them toward practices and policies that support ethics and security. A singular person or board can also evaluate emerging technologies and products in advance of their use to gauge potential ethical impact.

In some instances, companies have gone outside the organization for that oversight. Labeled by one company as its "guardian council," this particular outside board is an independent council whose members are experienced in data privacy and other related issues. This board is even empowered with authority to overrule management decisions that they worry may compromise ethics.[7] But no matter if it's in an actionable or advisory capacity, an outside board can prove very effective in providing helpful and objective guidance.

It's also advantageous to go outside your company regarding other steps. Given the absence of comprehensive legal guidelines in many cases, consider collaborating with others within your industry to build ethical frameworks for the use of emerging technologies.

But don't focus on such outside measures at the expense of attention to other steps toward building strong internal ethics. Consider measures to build a culture of ethical responsibility throughout the entire organization. Offer ongoing training and education to employees on current and effective practices regarding safety, responsibility, and the ethical application of technology.

Regarding the question of bias in AI technology, no go-to solution has yet to be discovered. But there are practical steps that can be taken, many of which are exclusively technical in nature. These include "pre-processing" data to minimize any relationship between outcomes and protected characteristics and the inclusion of extra data points to target bias-based outcomes.

Don't forget the human element. No math algorithm can accurately label what is "fair" and "unbiased." Doing so requires human judgment leveraging disciplines such as social sciences, law, and ethics to develop real-world standards.

Leaders can bring attention to the need to address machine bias with human intuition in other ways. Encourage leadership at all levels to weigh the significant benefits of an aspect of digital transformation against the possible ethical ramifications. In the end, fallout from an ethical misstep may far outweigh such desirable outcomes as revenue growth and market share.

Therein lies a particularly valuable benefit to ethical awareness. Think back to when you heard about a company or organization that had been hacked or accused of unethical behavior. That often placed a filter through which you and many others viewed that entity for some time to come.

That's where opportunity exists. How a company sees its ethical and security obligations can prove a powerful brand and market value differentiator. Companies that consciously go beyond requisite regulatory measures can be seen as good corporate citizens that truly embrace the significance of ethics, security, and other issues that can impact the buying public.

When it comes to ethics, going too far is never a bad idea. Bear that caveat in mind in your leadership, and your digital transformation will likely go more smoothly and, just as importantly, establish a genuine persona of trust that will engage customers, clients, and those within your organization.

NEED TO KNOW:

- To become an engaged leader amid your business's digital transformation, know the distinctions between digitization, digitalization, and digital transformation. They're significant.
- A pervasive digital mindset is critical to transform any organization digitally, taking in everyone from leadership all the way through the entire group. Such a mindset is comfortable with change and urges experimentation and occasional failure—which are necessary steps to success.
- Collaboration is essential, even connecting groups and people who may not have worked together before. But such synergy is essential, not merely to encourage a diversity of opinion and feedback but also to move away from autonomous silos that can inhibit transformational growth.
- Take steps to ensure that your culture not only has changed but is also built to last over time. Encourage a prevailing mindset of attention to the issue of sustainability: What policies and procedures are sustainable, as opposed to others that may be less resilient to change?
- Ethics are paramount. The public has seen more than enough security lapses, ethical misbehavior, and other instances to make them jumpy about technology in general. An emphasis on ethics makes regulatory sense—taking it further than you're required builds an appealing organizational persona, one that genuinely means what it says, rather than merely looking good.

CHAPTER 7

THE FUTURE OF YOUR ORGANIZATION

IN A SENSE, THIS chapter heading may seem a bit redundant.

After all, so much of the discussion up to this point makes the future an inherent aspect of everything to do with transforming your business—including a digital element. In particular, the issue of making *Transformation* sustainable underscores the importance of not only introducing digital components but also ensuring those components—as well as non-technical elements associated with *Transformation*—achieve their potential in years to come.

And that makes an understanding of what that future could likely entail a critical step in ensuring that digital transformation—and, as a result, the *Transformation* of an entire organization—does what you hope it does.

This swings back to a certain aspect of *Transformation* that may well fly under the radar for many leaders. First and foremost, *Transformation* that leverages digital technology doesn't make technology the exclusive focal point—in fact, it's anything but that. By its very nature, organizational *Transformation*—even if digital technology is a critical component—impacts almost everything, from the people involved in the effort to the culture that those people will work within moving forward.

Moreover, certain elements of that *Transformation* may be difficult to pinpoint, even though their impact may be significant. However subtle they may be, their influence can be both meaningful and far-reaching, potentially affecting your organization for many years ahead.

That's the purpose of a discussion about what your organization may look like once the mechanics of *Transformation* have come and gone. Examination of the scope and implications of change with a somewhat longer timeframe not only gives you a heads-up on what to anticipate but also allows you to make decisions today that will nurture the environment you hope to create for tomorrow—for all the tomorrows that follow.

ADDRESSING THE CUSTOMER EXPECTATIONS OF THE FUTURE—DIGITALLY

You certainly don't need any lectures about the overriding importance of customer service and satisfaction. That's been at the heart of any successful business well before the phrase "meeting customer expectations" was even coined.

Leadership knows that all too well. In one particular survey, 92 percent of leaders cited customer relationship management as a key priority for enabling their business strategy—so much so that it's routinely discussed at the board of directors' level.[1]

But that dynamic is changing in significant ways. Not only are consumers increasingly demanding in what they expect, but they're also taking a greater role in the development of all types of new products and services.

That ups the bar with respect to consumer satisfaction, and an important aspect of meeting those expectations is an appealing digital component.

In other words, it won't just be a question of addressing customers' needs in the future—it will also be an issue of doing so *digitally*. That's what a growing number of customers will both want and expect.

This isn't just a matter of consumers being more digitally savvy, although that's a significant element. In a trend that sharpened particularly during the COVID-19 pandemic, when customers shifted in enormous waves to online shopping, a broad swath of consumers have naturally become more comfortable using technology to research and make buying decisions—taking in everything from groceries to other consumer goods.

But that's not merely an issue of digital in and of itself. It's much more focused on all the benefits and possibilities that a digital consumer can enjoy. Waiting for a customer service representative to be available is no longer a necessary burden. Locating a particular product or type of service has become much more streamlined. Comparing that product with similar items is quick and reliable. Knowing when that product will be delivered is automatic and generally accurate.

As a result, when examining digital transformation, it's essential to consider the end consumers' digital experience—now and in the future. It's important to see this from your customers' viewpoint and work to create a connected experience that not merely satisfies customer priorities today but sufficiently adapts to achieve the same objective in the future.

Once again, bear in mind that most consumers don't see things the same way you do. You may believe your website grabs visitors and commands attention while, without hesitation, they jump from one digital channel to the next. To keep them with you, you need to give them a reason—increasingly expressed digitally—to stay there.

Accordingly, one study found that 29 percent of consumers want to see major improvements to the online resources that businesses provide. Further, 27 percent want to see a significant improvement to the buying process.[2] It's safe to say that those priorities will only grow in years to come.

Although that makes the digital experience a focal point of ongoing improvement, the components that go into identifying your digital needs—now and in the future—won't likely change much. You need—and will need—to attract customers to you. From there, they must navigate the digital process efficiently and gain exposure to those aspects of what you offer that separates you from others.

Additionally, once a purchase has taken place, it's critical to transform those customers into loyal advocates. And not merely cheerleaders—you want advocacy that fuels a willingness not only to spread the good word but also to return time and again for repeat purchases.

Moving forward, all those elements—technical as well as not—must be addressed digitally. And it's admittedly a long list, one that consumers will expect to experience sooner rather than later.

To meet the explosion of customer expectations, forward-thinking businesses need to look at digital transformation for solutions, not merely because digital can offer guidance and insight into strategies and possible answers but also because consumers will expect a top-tier experience that is delivered digitally—fast, insightful, and constantly adaptive.

One such digital solution lies in digital customer relationship management (CRM) software platforms. Stripped to the bare bones, CRM software is a system for managing customer relationships. CRM technology allows you to maintain a comprehensive record of different essential customer data points:

- *Consumer interactions*: website visits, phone and email contact, and other means of connection

- *Customer data*: buying preferences, inquiries, problems, and other pertinent issues

- *Subjective information*: notes from salespeople, marketers, and others with whom a consumer has had contact

Although it's certainly possible to maintain such information through a more manual form, keeping such records sufficiently updated can be a daunting challenge. More importantly, attempting to analyze such data in hopes of gaining comprehensive, viable insights can prove an equally time-consuming, arduous job.

Digital CRM steps into this breach nicely. First, CRM effectively automates data acquisition and management. A customer's initial contact with your CRM system might involve filling out a contact information form, signing up for a newsletter, or some other first step. Thereafter, additional data can be used to augment that information—browsing information, questions posed to either a digital system or a live customer service or sales representative, and other forms of informative contact. From there, any new data can be automatically added to the customer's portfolio, although a manual option may also be available.

Now is when digital CRM's potential really hits the gas with comprehensive, useful analysis. First, CRM is inherently efficient, as it provides a central source of readily available information. That data can be accessed by any number of people throughout an organization, including management, accounting, sales, marketing, and customer relationships.

That, in turn, makes effective personalization and related targeted outreach efforts that much more effective. With minimal or no effort on the part of an employee, a customer may receive a digital heads-up about an upcoming sale that includes past purchases. That same customer may also receive an automated follow-up after a purchase, not merely asking for feedback about the experience but also offering resources to get the most out of their purchase while proactively providing troubleshooting guidance.

Comprehensive knowledge of a customer's priorities and prior issues can prove particularly valuable when snafus occur. One particular way to improve this key element of customer service is through an electronic form of triage. Working with human employees, CRM can prioritize customers in terms of immediacy and complexity of the problem and, from there, refer them to employees best trained to address the issue. Even better, CRM's capacity to manage and analyze customer interactions can help circumvent future issues and complaints by helping your organization learn from past encounters.

When coupled with artificial intelligence, CRM can also digitalize processes in which no human is involved on either end. Here, using computer processors capable of sending and receiving data embedded in everyday objects, interaction can take place automatically. For instance, the "customer" might be a storage tank running low on fuel, which sends an automated message to the supplier requesting a refill.

That and other aspects of a new reality mandate digital immediacy. Customers want the best possible experiences offered through digital channels as quickly as possible. Using such tools as CRM, organizations of all types must not only introduce solutions applicable to today's customers' priorities but also commit to utilizing whatever resources necessary to arrive at solutions with the capacity to grow and adapt.

And, once again, that's a question of culture. Meeting the digital demands of tomorrow requires much more than a technological plug-and-play solution. A culture that prioritizes innovation, creativity, and thinking that run counter to precedent is necessary to, in effect, get in the game, win at the game, and change tactics as the rules of the game evolve, which they inevitably will.

GIVE A DIGITAL "KISS"

Transforming your business using digital technologies may seem complex. And in many ways it is, involving people at varied levels and skills, technology, timing, and the ever-prioritized issue of culture. Although, once we hit the third section in this book, where I walk you through the steps to make *Transformation* as systematic as possible, the journey may not seem quite so involved as it once might have.

But one challenge to address throughout the process is the goal of making what comes out in the end as relatively uncomplicated as possible. It can be a tough road to follow. By its very nature, adding more layers to existing tools and systems can make everything more difficult to parse and understand.

Obviously, one way to skirt the problem of layering is to replace as much legacy technology as possible with digital upgrades. That's one way to address the challenge of trying to make old technology and its much more current cousin complementary. Instead of going back and forth between existing systems and new tools, employees can focus on maximizing the potential that exists in more updated solutions.

That hits on an essential component of one core goal of *Transformation*—making certain that the work environment and mechanics resulting from *Transformation* with a digital element are as simple and straightforward as possible.

This might seem like a fairly lightweight epiphany, but it's nonetheless understandable to find yourself caught up in all the new technology at the potential expense of your people. For one thing, anything simple is that much easier to learn and master. Additionally, the more efficiently people work, the better the results for them, as well as for the entire organization. Further, the easier the mastery of new tools, the more people will be positioned to innovate, create, and have the confidence to approach their work in a different, unhindered manner.

The same holds true for consumers. Not even the most tech-giddy customer wants to put up with a website or digital customer service system that's difficult to navigate. According to a poll conducted by digital experience company Acquia, when asked what they care about most when interacting with a brand online, 65 percent of consumers said, "A website that's easy to find what I want," over "Interesting content" and "A brand's social media presence."[3]

So, look to ensure that what emerges from your organization's transformation follows the old acronym of "KISS"—that is, "Keep it simple, stupid." Ultimately, steps to simplify your digital reinvention will make the last word in that catchphrase utterly moot.

THE FUTURE—DO YOUR JOB, THEN LEAVE

By this point in our discussion, digital transformation and disruption have become inextricably intertwined.

Staffing and management of personnel are no exception—yet another aspect of the future to bear in mind. That's because traditional staffing parameters may not jibe with a digitally driven environment.

For one thing, it's a completely different ballgame when it comes to the challenges of the technology. Finding appropriately trained, skilled talent to work with new technology such as advanced analytics, robotic process automation, and other responsibilities can be challenging itself—particularly so if the focus is exclusively on hiring full-time, in-house professionals.

Many business leaders are increasingly receptive toward a strategic and flexible staffing model that's more fitting for a digital age. This strategy includes a mix of permanent employees—many of whom can direct most of their efforts to initiatives critical to the organization—and skilled contract professionals who support them and provide highly specific expertise, often on an "as-needed" basis.

That can help in two distinct ways. First, by retaining a core of full-time, permanent employees, organizations can continue to groom career personnel—a task that can be particularly challenging in an intensely competitive labor market. Meanwhile, the use of outsiders in a more specific manner allows organizations to better handle technological issues and the challenges of *Transformation* without the expense of hiring full-timers. This flexibility lends both internal stability and the cost-efficient capacity to adjust quickly.

This approach doesn't have to be limited to individuals. Digitally driven businesses are increasingly farming out short-term needs to subcontractors, which, like individual employees, do what they're charged to do and then move on. For instance, a number of Italian auto manufacturers, having undergone varied degrees of digital transformation, use varied subcontractors for highly specific jobs in the manufacturing process, such as particular features in certain car models.

As an aside, it's not coincidental that the Italian auto industry is something of a poster child for the benefits of digital transformation. In 2017, Italy introduced the Industry 4.0 National Plan, a government program to help companies capitalize on rapidly shifting technology. The initiative allowed companies to choose from a wide variety of incentives to transition to more digitized factories and other steps to leverage technological growth. As a result, Italy has been at the forefront of high-tech manufacturing in Europe and the world. Further, projections hold that the nation's automakers will recover from the impact of COVID-19 much faster than other sectors of Italy's economy.

Overall, greater flexibility in the future will also encompass greater levels of collaboration. Just as digitally transformed organizations will use so-called outsiders for varied needs, firms will increasingly partner with a number of entities, including suppliers, research organizations, customers, and even competitors. With the overriding mindset that it's better to partner than compete so that everyone benefits, collaboration will focus on improving distribution, broadening product lines, and boosting manufacturing flexibility and capacity. Further, by sharing research and market awareness, firms can also drive innovation with greater collaboration.

ADDRESS INTERNAL ANXIETIES

Leaders whose organizations are about to embark on a digital transformation or are already well on their way are all too familiar with the rattled nerves of employees who fear their jobs will be axed due to the introduction of a digital environment. Sorry to say, but angst doesn't necessarily go away once the *Transformation* has taken hold.

It can boil down to a lose-lose dynamic. A *Transformation* that fails for any number of reasons—for example, insufficient buy-in of employees—is viewed as a respite. No *Transformation*, no pink slip. On the other side, a digital transformation that takes hold and prospers is viewed as a growing threat, one whose development can seem to threaten human workers with no end in sight.

I address this issue earlier in the book, but it bears a return visit because it's likely going to be just as much a concern for an organization's future. Accordingly, it's critical for leaders to recognize those fears—and to stress that digital transformation is not a job killer, but rather an opportunity for employees to upgrade their skills and experience to complement the shifting nature of their industry and the overall marketplace.

Start by encouraging a mindset in which employee activities are aligned with digital transformation, rather than colliding with it. Ask your employees to pinpoint what specifically they bring to the organization and the connection those attributes have with elements of digital transformation. For instance, challenge a talented sales team to identify how digital tools can help them better manage leads, sales, and follow-up. Stress that, rather than shoving them to the curb, digital technology can help make them better at something they're already skilled in doing.

This strategy affords employees an element of control and a greater comfort level with how digital transformation will take hold. Also, continue to emphasize this personal commitment to innovation as the organization moves forward. As digital transformation never truly ends, so too should a focus on continually evolving and improving to complement that shifting environment never cease.

Other strategies to mitigate pervasive technophobia in tomorrow's organization include the following:

- Look to create agile work assignments and responsibilities. The greater the variety of work, the better the chances of identifying a component that can be nurtured within a digital setting.

- Maintain flexibility . . . and more flexibility. Akin to using outsiders, don't be shy about moving people around internally to address both organizational needs and work skills. For example, borrow from another department or swap out people completely to compensate for a lack of a given digital skill. Adjust roles to realign with what's required in a new environment.

- Remember that digital tools can, in fact, make some human skills replaceable. Even though some roles can be adapted to a digital environment, not every job is completely immune. One option is to maintain the job as it is for the time being while keeping an eye out for future development that may threaten the position. If possible, adapt or enhance the existing role wherever possible. However, it may be necessary to eliminate the job completely should digital transformation make the existing position unsupportable.

- Bear in mind, though, that getting rid of the role doesn't have to involve getting rid of the talent. If a job is axed, look for other opportunities for gifted employees—perhaps involving additional training or the creation of a completely new job, one less vulnerable to a changing work environment. Eliminating a job doesn't necessarily mean cutting talented employees loose.

- Continue to empower digital innovation—everywhere. When it comes to championing innovation, don't limit your focus to people and jobs that may prove vulnerable to digital transformation. Instead, emphasize ongoing innovation as a mainstay of your responsibilities moving forward. Innovation mandates open communication, collaboration, and the freedom to experiment and create. Offer both the tools and environment to allow employees to continue to imagine, develop, and implement new skills, new ideas, and new processes that complement a digital driver.

A DIFFERENT KIND OF VALUE

Some observers have pointed out that, as digital transformation takes hold, organizations must stop *doing digital* and start *being digital*. That can have a significant financial impact, both on where your finances are allocated and on how you define value.

To start with, a proactive approach to digital transformation means committing financially to investment and development opportunities in new tools and platforms to improve the customer experience. That may also require a different view of ROI for technology initiatives—although specifics will differ from one setting to another, it's beneficial to make realistic estimates in terms of payoff, as well as the timeframe involved. As has been stressed, *Transformation* using digital technology is a journey—likely a long, ongoing one. While positive ROI is essential to reinforce the confidence of all stakeholders, don't necessarily expect too much too soon.

Additionally, the future of *Transformation* may also suggest a different view of what defines company value and, further, how it's generated.

Formerly, firm value was associated with tangible assets, as well as such barometers as the amount of revenue each employee generated. But, moving forward—as is the case with so many other aspects of *Transformation*—value is also defined by external value creation involving external partnerships.

Known in one respect as an "inverted firm," well-known examples of external value creation include such behemoths as Google and Facebook, neither of which create posts or webpages. Likewise, Apple doesn't write most of the apps it happily sells. Amazon makes only a fraction of the goods it offers. Various studies have confirmed that the sort of growth enjoyed by such icons can also be captured by considerably smaller organizations.

Typically speaking, organizations transforming digitally are focused on making things on the inside work better. And that's a perfectly valid objective. But acquiring newly defined value that also derives from the outside involves a coordinated, nurturing relationship with external partners, including suppliers, developers, those involved in supply chains, and customers. Over time, all parties involved contribute to the growth in value of everyone.

To attract and cement relationships with value-creating external collaborators, bear in mind the simple rule of creating more value than you take. Focus on overall value creation, rather than drooling after a bigger slice of the pie. Take what steps you need to help partners grow as you do.

Although the specifics of what tools to offer external partners will vary according to needs and circumstances, one possible choice is known as *permissioning* technology. Here, external partners can access your internal resources under carefully monitored parameters. This not only allows partners to leverage what you can give them more efficiently but also cements a greater sense of quid pro quo—sharing what resources you choose to control while also accessing resources under the purview of others, which increases overall value for all involved.

All this mandates an approach to leadership that many executives must work on—a type of leadership this book examines. To a very large degree, you will have to rely on external partners' willingness to proactively share ideas and resources they have that you do not. This isn't an outsourcing arrangement, where you specify what you need and someone else supplies it. Instead, an element of trust must be in place, along with an environment that promotes that sort of essential trust.

That takes a leader who doesn't micromanage, who boosts outside collaboration rather than looking to control it through mandate. Moreover, it requires a common mindset of sharing, not greedily grabbing for all you can reach to your sole benefit.

That ties in with the overall theme of this particular chapter—that *Transformation* will impact your organization in the future in ways that might surprise you. *Transformation* with a digital component merely begins with the technology itself—the ramifications for the future are much broader than that, requiring organizational structure, culture, and leadership that, in its own way, is just as transformative as the digital transformation itself.

SECTION 3

SECTION 3

WHAT TO DO:
NAVIGATING WITH LIFTS

AS IF THE TECHNICAL elements to digital transformation weren't intimidating enough, the challenges posed by introducing a suitable culture at the same time might make the whole process seem insurmountable.

Luckily, that is far from the case.

As we've examined, organizational *Transformation* that includes a digital element isn't simply a matter of plugging in all the shiny new tools and flicking on a switch. What undermines many attempts at *Transformation* is insufficient attention to everything else that has to change as well. That means, in many cases, sweeping cultural reinvention—taking in everything from specifically identifying what you hope to achieve via your *Transformation* to acclimating everyone within the organization to new ways of seeing, doing, and managing issues within the parameters of broad change.

That may seem like a lot—and, truth be told, it is. If nothing else, it's a somewhat vulnerable process—if one element of your effort at *Transformation* stumbles, the entire initiative can be compromised or potentially scuttled.

That's where the acronym LIFTS comes in. LIFTS stands for the following five steps:

1. L—Learn
2. I—Investigate
3. F—Formulate
4. T—Take off
5. S—Study

Those steps, which are arranged in the order in which they should be implemented, are much more than a slight variant of my prior book *LIFT* (couldn't resist the plug). Rather, they're an easy way to remember the systematic methodology to help you prepare, navigate, and leverage your organizational *Transformation*.

1. *Learn*: This step begins with defining a common definition of what *Transformation* means to your organization. As I address shortly, a critical element of a successful transformative initiative is obtaining a complete level of buy-in from everyone impacted by the *Transformation*. To obtain that to the greatest extent possible, a clear understanding of strategy is essential—not just an understanding of how individual roles will be affected, but also what the *Transformation* means to the organization as a whole. Additionally, the learning step involves the idea of value discipline—the core advantage the organization hopes to achieve through *Transformation*. Finally, take the time to appreciate the scope of impact of technology with regard to reinvention—the many ways processes, procedures, and even ways of thinking will be reshaped. Reinvention can be intimidating to many—the greater the understanding, the lower the anxiety.

2. *Investigate*: Next up is investigation—more specifically, an assessment of potential areas where digital transformation affords specific opportunities. This can include financial, functional, social, and other areas of potential. This enables you to pinpoint areas of possible benefit that could warrant particular attention and resources. Regarding that potential, the investigation stage boils down to three basic components:

   ○ *Organization*: What organizational structure exists that can impact your planned *Transformation*, and are you ready for the *Transformation* itself?

   ○ *External*: Which outside forces might also influence *Transformation*?

   ○ *Risk*: How have significant changes in technology broadened the focus of risk management from the micro-project view to a much wider perspective?

   By taking all three considerations into account, you're preparing your organization to begin the actual implementation of *Transformation* with genuine confidence in your own capabilities, as well as in potential problem areas.

3. *Formulate*: Here you'll be introduced to portfolio and program management (PPM)—concepts that allow you to better understand assets and activities and to ensure that every element of your *Transformation* receives an appropriate level of support. As you'll see, PPM provides top managers a centralized and balanced view of the payoffs of various projects while also highlighting risks and particular challenges.

4. *Take off*: It's time for your *plan and launch*. This is a comprehensive, ongoing process designed to develop and begin the overall digital transformation process. It's important to closely monitor

initial progress, considering such factors as projected costs, schedule, performance, and expected business benefits. Concepts such as strategic enterprise architecture can be used to better manage and coordinate activities. This section also takes an additional look at specific definitions and implications of technology and effective ways to track change and overall progress.

5. *Study*: Finally, assess how everything is coming along, as well as your progress toward previously identified goals. This section encompasses the development and use of appropriate metrics with which such objectives can be measured. In particular, the issue of agility will be emphasized as *Transformation* moves forward, requiring ongoing monitoring and adjustments. As you'll learn, one key goal is the creation of an information-oriented culture, one whose operation is in sync with new technology and the different dynamics brought about by *Transformation*.

One essential thought to bear in mind as we move toward discussion of a systematic methodology is that, in so many words, the LIFTS approach incorporates science as well as art. On one hand, I suggest specific ideas and strategies that I believe are, at the very least, worthy of consideration for any organization approaching sweeping *Transformation*. But it's not a lecture that should necessarily be followed verbatim. Since you and your team know the particulars of your situation far better than anyone else, it's up to you to pick and choose those ideas and actions that best fit your situation. The optimal approach is more à la carte than a defined menu—I offer possible ingredients, but it falls on you to devise the specific recipe that works best for you.

Moreover, take things in a prudent, sensible chronology. As the old saying goes, you need to crawl first, then walk, and ultimately run. As you will see, in addition to recommended steps and ideas, I also touch on the capabilities of your organization—what you can do very well and those things that you need to sharpen. Approach my methodology with capability in the back of your mind. Steps toward *Transformation* work only if you're genuinely capable of taking them. Accordingly, I try to help you along the way by highlighting points at which your assessment of what your organization can truly do will prove essential in successfully implementing what I believe are effective steps toward a successful reinvention.

Let's have a closer look at the five steps of LIFTS.

CHAPTER 8

LEARN

TAKE A MOMENT TO recall an experience in your life when you felt you were "out of the loop" while everyone around you was fully clued in to what was taking place and why, and you were left pretty much in the dark—confused and perhaps not just a little upset.

Not a good feeling at all. That's why the very first step in implementing a transformative process in your organization is to educate everyone impacted by the effort.

But that needs to involve much more than a cursory overview. Rather, it's critical that every stakeholder in the transformative effort has a comprehensive understanding and appreciation for varied elements of the *Transformation*, as well as of the objectives and possible problems. That way, you're able to build a united and informed team—one with as complete a buy-in as possible to work toward the best results attainable.

BE SPECIFIC—WHAT'S THE BUSINESS STRATEGY?

Start with establishing a common definition of what *Transformation* means to your organization or company. Although the term may hint at complete reinvention, what that effort actually involves will naturally differ from one organization to another. It's helpful to be as specific as possible. For instance, if you're looking toward faster, more responsive customer service, what exactly does "faster" mean? Can that be quantified? What does "more responsive" imply? Is that simply a matter of speed or of substance? The more you can hammer down commonly accepted and understandable terms, the more your teammates will recognize not only what is being discussed but also how their roles may apply to the issue at hand.

As has been noted earlier, the term *digital transformation* is used so often that its meaning is often misconstrued or misunderstood. Accordingly, stakeholder education should focus on a clear, readily understandable definition explaining what digital transformation means to your organization—one that's as closed to interpretation as possible. Avoid use of insider terminology or jargon—not only can that be confusing (resulting in that dreaded "outside the loop" feeling), but it may also prove utterly inaccurate. A team member who mistakenly sees digital transformation as focused on one area, when in fact other aspects of the organization are also impacted, may inadvertently hinder progress—or worse, make others around them just as confused.

That's where specific business strategy comes in. This defines the strategic goals, imperatives, and initiatives that the organization is pursuing, including those specific business capabilities that make it all happen. The following four-step process helps you direct your thinking about digital technology investments for *Transformation*.[1]

It's an important exercise. Defining and selecting business capabilities are the most critical decisions an organization can make regarding digital technology investments. Selecting the right capabilities is also very complex, requiring a thorough analysis of the business.

TECHNOLOGY INVESTMENT DECISION-MAKING

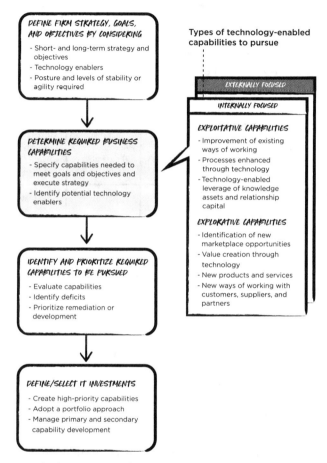

Figure 8.1. Technology investment decision-making process.[2] *Determining investments must begin with a solid understanding of an organization's strategy, goals, and objectives.*

Organizations need to examine how they will use digital technology to enable strategic actions. This is illustrated in Figure 8.2 for four classes of technology investments: transactions, decisions, intellectual capital, and relationships.

ENABLING STRATEGIC ACTIONS

AREA	TRANSACTION FOCUSED	DECISION FOCUSED	INTELLECTUAL CAPITAL FOCUSED	RELATIONSHIP FOCUSED
Definition	Enhances the quality of ongoing transactions	Enhances the quality of ongoing decisions	Enhances the quality of organizational intelligence	Enhances the quality of relationships across the firm and across the extended enterprise
Exploitative Strategic Actions	- Speed - Reliability - Volume - Cost	- Speed - Volume - Completeness - Reliability	- Codifiability - Accessibility - Transferability	- Reach - Velocity - Depth - Customization
Explorative Strategic Actions	- Reach - Breadth - Visibility	- Distributed - Multiple perspectives - Local autonomy	- Reach - Breadth - Distributed - Multiple perspectives	- Adaptability - Breadth

Figure 8.2. Enabling strategic actions through digital technology.[3] Organizations exploit four types of investments to support strategic positions.

Transaction-focused investment enables transactions (both within an enterprise and with external parties) to occur faster and more reliably with fewer errors or steps. That boosts productivity and responsiveness while lowering costs. Transaction-focused investment also encourages exploration by increasing both the number of potential parties with whom transactions can be executed and the potential types of transactions that can be handled. Additionally, transactions throughout the organization become more visible, which is extremely important today with most organizations finding themselves forced to share data about key business events—orders, deliveries, low inventory levels—with customers or suppliers who are expecting their strategic partners to do the same. With increased information visibility across supply chains and value nets, business models and value propositions that were unimaginable only a few years ago have become the norm.

Decision-focused investment enables decision automation. This occurs by embedding decision rules within software and providing employees with enhanced information and proven filters for decision situations that are not automated. Decisions are made faster, more reliably, and more completely, thus increasing decision quality and responsiveness, as well as employee productivity. This lowers costs and better aligns products and services with customer requirements. Decision-focused investment also expands decision authority by increasing the number of perspectives brought to bear on a decision and by allowing more discretion to employees closest to a decision. Emerging opportunities are more likely to be recognized, interpreted from a variety of perspectives, and acted on.

Intellectual capital–focused investment focuses on the best use of knowledge and information that has been acquired and created. Valuable data is embedded in processes and decision-making and distributed more widely throughout the organization. Leveraging this information regarding the organization's product and markets, as well as the assets and activities needed to enhance strategic positions in them, produces more consistent thought, purpose, and ability across the organization. Intellectual capital–focused investment also boosts an organization's "intelligence at the edge" by increasing the number and variety of accessible external sources of knowledge, increasing organization-wide visibility into what is happening at the organization's edges, and enabling specialized knowledge sources to be easily established, promoted, and accessed.

Relationship-focused investment strengthens relationships across an organization and with trusted partners. On the inside, it provides collaborative work environments in which the insight of all employees involved in crafting a strategic position can be brought to bear without regard for time, location, or positions. Externally, it creates resilient links with partners that enable the firm's ability to work with them and understand them better. Relationship-focused investment also makes it easier to form or disband partnerships. As a result, a breadth of assets, skills, and competencies becomes available to identify, assess, and act on opportunities. Just as important, those associated with underperforming positions can be reassigned or eliminated.

To illustrate the many different roles served by digital technology and supporting investments, consider the action initiated by Herman Miller in the late 1990s to stake a strategic position in an underserved market—that of offering small businesses no-frills, quality furnishings delivered quickly at a reasonable price. In accomplishing this strategic initiative, Miller established a new operating unit, Herman Miller SQA (Simple, Quick, and Affordable), and introduced a flurry of innovations that have since migrated into the parent company:

- Local dealers are provided with innovative 3D visualizing tools and product configurators that are used in consulting with customers about a potential order—furniture, design styles, fabrics, wood finishes, space layout, and so on (incorporating decision- intellectual capital–, and relationship-focused technology investments).

- When the dealer and customer have reached agreement on an order, the software creates an order list with all parts and the final price (decision- and transaction-focused investments).

- As soon as an order is accepted, it is sent via the internet to a Miller SQA manufacturing facility, where it enters production and logistics scheduling systems. Within two hours, the dealer and customer receive confirmation of delivery and installation dates (decision-, relationship-, and transaction-focused investments).

- Finally, Miller SQA's supply net transparently links its many suppliers to its operations, streamlining purchasing, inventory, and production processes. Here, the 500 suppliers can access data in Miller SQA's systems, allowing them to automatically send more materials when needed (decision-, relationship-, intellectual capital–, and transaction-focused investments). This use of digital technology allowed Miller SQA to reduce an industry order cycle of about fourteen weeks to about two—and in the process redefined what was required for competitive success in this product-market niche.[4]

At first glance, the Herman Miller example belies the notion that technology assets are, for the most part, commodities. However, with a deeper look, it becomes clear that digital investment wasn't the only reason behind such success. Firm-specific structure and content embedded within business architectures also helped business strategies to unfold, aided by a well-honed set of strategic business management.

CREATE CULTURE THAT INCLUDES VALUE DISCIPLINE

Value discipline refers to the primary advantage the company seeks to achieve in the marketplace. The choice of a value discipline shapes the company's subsequent strategies and underlying operating model. Using a model developed by Michael Treacy and Fred Wiersema in *The Discipline of Market Leaders*,[5] leading companies keep their edges by selecting one discipline and emphasizing it. Following are some examples:

- *Customer intimacy*: Cultivating close and long-term customer relationships requires intimate knowledge of customer needs and priorities, creating a dependency of customized service and support and an ongoing focus on retention and satisfaction. According to Treacy and Wiersema, a company that delivers value through customer intimacy does not deliver what the market wants, but rather what a specific customer wants. Therefore, the company's greatest asset is its customer loyalty.

- *Operational excellence*: This discipline offers a combination of quality, price, and ease of purchase that no one else in the market can match. The focus is on solid execution, guaranteed low prices, hassle-free services, standardizing, and simplifying. Operationally excellent companies not only promise the lowest total cost, according to Treacy and Wiersema, but are able to do it 365 days a year.

- *Product leadership*: Here, the emphasis is on innovation and development of products that push performance boundaries. The organization invents, develops, and markets with tremendous speed, making its own products obsolete. A product leader's proposition to customers, according to Treacy and Wiersema, is the best product—period!

Value type refers to the nature of the value that a company seeks to create. There are stability and agility dimensions to value. Stability refers to the extent to which operations can be made efficient, effective, and predictable. Agility refers to the extent to which the organization can identify new opportunities and seize them by responding appropriately.[6]

VALUE DISCIPLINES

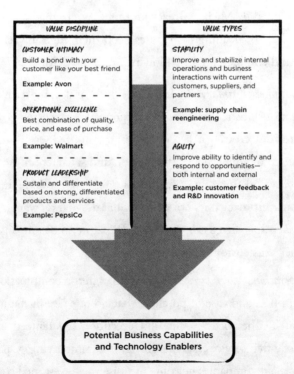

Figure 8.3. Value disciplines and value types.[7] Organizations focus on selected value disciplines and seek to create corresponding value types.

BUSINESS AND TECHNOLOGY CAPABILITIES

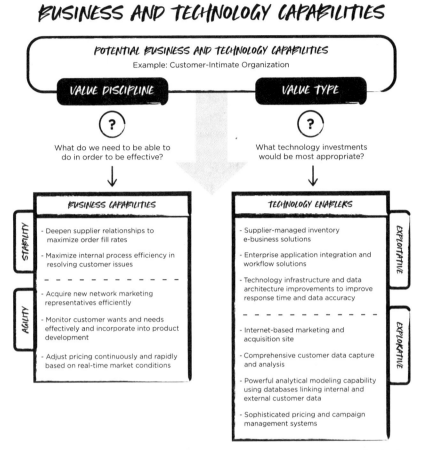

Figure 8.4. Potential business and technology capabilities.[8] Business capabilities and technology enablers are derived from decisions about an organization's value discipline and value type.

Initiatives undertaken by the delivery company DHL provide a good illustration of technology-enabled exploitative capabilities for value creation. DHL, in seeking its own version of exploitative capabilities, focused on integrating technology with its knowledge and relationship assets. It adopted a web-based solution that enables agents, partners, managers, and other users to maintain a single view of all customer information, gain instant access to organizational knowledge, and efficiently interact with customers across multiple communication channels, leading to vastly improved capabilities in customer service. Similarly, 3M invested in creating online access through its corporate intranet to the company's enormous volume of customer content. As a result, 3M now has superior capability to service its customers, who no longer need to wait while service representatives research their inquiries and issues.

EMPHASIZE THE BREADTH OF IMPACT OF TECHNOLOGY

Digital technology has the potential to shape the four roles of business strategy.

Automation: Here, technology applies to transaction and work process automation that enables higher productivity and efficiency and lower cost. Automation also makes conducting business easier, where employees, customers, or business partners can access services with speed, convenience, and personalization. Examples include deployment of customer self-service (self-checkouts at retail stores, online check-in for airlines), employee self-service (desktop-based self-procurement, self-management of benefits), and online sales. These and other steps boost signals that the firm's focus is on seamless enterprise and inter-enterprise services, global process connectivity, and the quest for ever-increasing digitization. Key business value metrics focus on productivity (inventory turnover), cycle time (to fulfill orders), and costs.

Empowerment: The role of technology here is to facilitate fast, effective, and accurate decision-making across the enterprise and its partnership network. This is accomplished through investments in decision support tools and technologies (for example, data warehousing, data mining), intranets for dissemination of best practices, and extranets for rapid sharing of information with business partners. Empowerment also makes business easier by providing front-end workers with intelligence and decision support in their interactions with customers, business partners, or

STRATEGIC ROLES FOR BUSINESS OPTIONS

STRATEGIC ROLE	DESCRIPTION	BUSINESS VALUE METRICS
Automation	Target transaction and work process automation to improve the productivity and ease with which the organization conducts its business	- Productivity (e.g., inventory turnover) - Cycle time (e.g., fulfillment cycle time) - Costs (e.g., procurement costs)
Empowerment	Provide information, decision support, and "best practice" knowledge to front-end workers in their interactions with customers, business partners, or other external stakeholders	- Partner satisfaction (e.g., customer satisfaction) - Problem resolution productivity (e.g., number of problems resolved, cycle time to resolution) - Resolution costs (e.g., cost per customer call)
Control	Facilitate efficient and real-time monitoring of business operations and business partners	- Completeness, accuracy, validity, and integrity of the firm's transactions and decision-making processes - Accuracy, speed, and economy of financial reporting - Effectiveness of financial audits and fraud detection
Transformation	Facilitate the innovation of new business models, new products and services, and new modes of organizing work	- Rate of product, process, or business model innovation - Comprehensiveness and richness of innovation portfolio (number of incremental, architectural, and radical innovations)

Figure 8.5. Four strategic roles for business options.[9] Technology helps shape business strategy and enables business options through four strategic roles.

other external stakeholders. Many of these interactions require problem or dispute resolution. This can be addressed with decision support scripts for call centers and customer service agents and visibility tools in supply chain and logistics processes.

Control: Technology can also facilitate efficient and real-time monitoring of business operations and business partners through practices such as daily operational alerts and dashboards with drill-down capabilities. This is achieved through investments in monitoring tools and technologies (for example, data warehouses, portals) and through the design of enterprise risk management processes. Control enables the business goals of enhancing transparency of business operations, rapid detection and resolution of management control issues, and accurate reporting of the key metrics of business performance. Key business value metrics include the completeness, accuracy, validity, and integrity of the firm's transactions and decision-making processes; the accuracy, speed, and economy of financial reporting; and the effectiveness of financial audits and fraud detection.

Transformation: This role of technology is to support innovation of new business models (for example, direct-to-customer, multiple-channel integration, whole of the enterprise or "one face" integration, value net integration), new products and services (digital products and services, digitized customer service through online chats), and new modes of organizing work (globally distributed work practices). The focus here is not so much on investment in specific technologies as it is on the development of digital options, digitization of products and services, and experimentation with new technology-enabled business ideas. *Transformation* enables the business goals of continuous innovation, agility, and competitive disruption. Key business value metrics include the rate of product, process, or business model innovation and the comprehensiveness and richness of a firm's innovation portfolio (number of incremental, architectural, and radical innovations).

ORGANIZE, COMMUNICATE, MANAGE

Articulating a strategic vision about the role of technology is a significant element of strategic governance. Strategic vision must capture and reflect three realities:

All organizations apply technology in all four of the strategic roles previously listed. In crafting a strategic vision, the key is to make clear the relative dominance of each role for the enterprise.

1. An organization's various units will likely exhibit differences regarding the relative importance of these four roles. Such unit differences must be accounted for in developing processes, organization structures, and information requirements and deploying automating technology.

2. Business environments, technology, and management teams are always in flux. Thus, while firms might choose a specific vision today, over time, such a vision is likely to change, perhaps dramatically.

At a time when technology spending is no longer an administrative overhead but a source of both top-line growth and bottom-line savings, executives must develop an appreciation of how specific investments impact key metrics of firm performance. For instance, Blue Shield of California is a not-for-profit organization that provides health insurance for 2.7 million members, generating $7 billion in annual revenues. From the perspective of the chief financial officer, technology impacts two key areas: analytics (the ability to price health-care plan offerings) and services operations (such as claims payment, eligibility, and enrollment). This firm views the value of its technology investments through the lens of operational efficiency, customer service, and pricing effectiveness.

The necessity of consistent language segues nicely into a related element. First, it's valuable to structure your entire organization with an ongoing focus on communication and learning. Committees and other actionable groups should be established not merely to execute when the time comes but to make certain that everyone impacted by change is informed, involved, and sufficiently prepared to carry out their varied responsibilities with clarity and understanding. From there, make certain that communication involving varied groups and stakeholders—both vertically and horizontally—is ongoing, consistent, and straightforward, not "dumbed down" but rather understandable and on point.

These and other elements fall under the umbrella title of "change management." Change management is not so much a strategy as it is an essential expertise. In other words, don't let change simply happen—direct and control it to the greatest extent possible. Through organization and communication, you'll be able to steer initiatives and impact outcomes better than with an approach that is less structured and more hands-off. That's not to recommend anything that hints at micromanagement—it's anything but that. Instead, work toward a level of ongoing awareness and attention to directing change with support, candor, and transparency.

With regard to digital transformation, this approach simply makes a world of sense. Digital transformation is imposing and intimidating and can jump the proverbial rail at any number of points—the type of pervasive risk that comes from something so comprehensive. The more effective the rudder that guides the journey, the more consistent the progress, as well as the capability for flexibility to make any midcourse adjustments.

Not only should change management arrive at and implement sensible decisions; it should also have a sense of a reasonable timeframe in which to introduce elements of change. Rushing the process can be disastrous, as the candy manufacturer Hershey's can attest to. Although the confectionary giant invested enormous sums of money and resources, it moved too quickly to implement the entire system—once one problem cropped up as a result, the resulting falling domino effect caused problems throughout the initiative. An additional mistake was attempting to implement the transformation during the holiday season, when chocolate and other sweets are in particularly high demand.[10]

INDIVIDUAL BENEFITS

However important, noble goals that impact the entire organization shouldn't be the only explanation for digital reinvention. Another way to build teammate support and buy-in is to appeal to self-benefit. How will people's lives—professional or personal—become better as a result of all this *Transformation* you're talking about? It's all well and good to point out how the organization stands to grow and improve, but what about the individuals who make that organization what it is? Just what do they stand to receive from all this upheaval, occasional uncertainty, perhaps not infrequent anxiety, and, ultimately, change from which there is almost certainly no turning back?

Not surprisingly, this may seem to be a highly specific challenge. After all, what's going to be of value to people in sales may be utterly inapplicable to technical support. Look to hit group and individual sweet spots to highlight specific benefits that may only apply to them. If accounting has a specific benefit on the horizon, emphasize it. Personal and group gain are powerful motivators.

That said, however, watch for connective and correlative benefits as well. Just because one area of the organization stands to receive a particular boost by way of *Transformation* doesn't mean that others will also enjoy a concomitant payout. As I've discussed, digital transformation can literally reinvent marketing by identifying trends, related responses, and patterns that can suggest future action. That's great, but if marketing gets a shot in the arm, doesn't that suggest greater results for your salesforce? If marketing is constantly ramping up its activities, won't your graphic design people also notice a related jump in workloads? Could that, in turn, lead to new hires or simply better job security? Be sure to play up all the benefits that cross departmental lines and areas of responsibility.

EMPHASIZE AUTONOMY, CREATIVITY, COLLABORATION

When a significant initiative involving broad change is implemented, it's understandable for many people to approach the new environment with a good dose of wariness. That has to do with leadership's view of just how hands-on things should be moving forward.

The question is, if everything is changing as much as it is, will management go overboard in monitoring how the organization performs? Will "Big Brother" keep his eye on me to gauge how I'm doing with new tools within a very different environment than what I'm used to?

Again, that's not hard to fathom. Any time an organization opts to shift gears in some manner or another, it's easy to see how people might worry that management may be looking at everyone with a particularly keen, if not critical, eye. That can be particularly true in organizations with a legacy of close management control—when things are new, people accustomed to tight control may feel the noose of micromanagement constricting even tighter.

Make certain to address this concern as a central element of your teammates' education regarding *Transformation*. One of the most appealing benefits of organizational *Transformation* with a digital component is greater autonomy. In one respect, since digital technology applied successfully can limit repetitive tasks and other forms of workplace drudgery, people will find they have greater freedom to craft their work experience to their liking and in a manner that they feel makes them most productive.

As is already noted, another plus to digital transformation is greater transparency and dissemination of information. As digital tools promote greater interaction and involvement throughout the organization, teammates at all levels are naturally better informed and equipped to make decisions and choices without undue management oversight.

That can occur on an individual level as well as in a team setting. For instance, having instituted an extensive array of digital platforms to maintain accountability without traditional managerial monitoring, appliance manufacturer Haier's thousands of employees effectively manage themselves. Workers are organized into more than 4,000 microenterprises that each manage their own profits and losses, hire and fire their own members, and decide which other microenterprises to collaborate with.[11]

Greater autonomy, in turn, leads to greater creativity—a core attribute of the evolving workplace setting. With time freed up as a result of digital automation, greater access to helpful data and technology, and other benefits, workers will naturally enjoy greater latitude in what they work on and how.

Not only does that open the door to new and innovative solutions and ideas, but it also promotes employee growth in both a personal and professional sense. In an environment focused on creativity, employees can obtain new hard and soft skills, as well as grow personal self-confidence. And that's a benefit not just limited to the individual. Employees who enjoy their work but also embrace beneficial learning opportunities tend to be more content to remain in their jobs. That can help address the nagging issue of employee retention for many companies.

An environment of collaboration is equally attractive. As digital technology empowers individuals and teams and allows greater interaction with others with whom they may have never worked before, the synergy derived from rewarding collaboration boosts creativity, cooperation, and a feeling of shared mission—an autonomous, creative organization that's comfortably in sync with itself.

UNDERSTAND WHAT THEY'RE NERVOUS ABOUT

For many, *Transformation* with a digital aspect is an exciting prospect, filled with possibilities and potential.

For just as many, it's a source of fear and anxiety. And a core component of educating your employees and colleagues about *Transformation* is working to address and eliminate as much nervous uncertainty as possible.

Many fears are touched on earlier in this book: Fear of too much disruption. Fear of being replaced by technology. Fear that expansive new technology will only prompt management to exert greater control over the workforce.

Complete, comprehensive education is the best remedy for all the concern. From a global perspective, the more everyone knows just what *Transformation* involves and how everyone will be impacted, the greater the potential comfort level, as well as the willingness to accept and embrace everything new.

For instance, having just addressed the issue of greater individual and team autonomy, people in management positions may experience some jitters about their own futures. After years of dutifully climbing the leadership ladder to a desired level, it's not hard to understand why those in certain leadership positions may feel threatened by a change that, at least to them, reduces and even eliminates the need for human direction.

That can be addressed through a variety of avenues. First, point out that it's realistic to accept that, no matter the level of autonomy, technology cannot make every decision that a living human being can. Colloquially, "calls from the gut" will always have a place in any organization, based on such factors as personal relationships, emotions, and other issues that machines simply cannot consider.

Moreover, not every individual in an organization is necessarily going to embrace greater autonomy. For whatever reason, there's no shortage of talented employees who welcome a degree of oversight, if for no other reason than as a form of helpful feedback and guidance. Put simply, lots of people like having a boss around.

Additionally, point out that greater autonomy is a two-way street.

Just as others gain time and freedom to do things that were formerly beyond their reach, so too can management leverage more professional freedom. That could mean opportunities for continuing education, the addition of new skills, or simply time to approach their work with a greater sense of freedom and innovation.

However, to broaden the discussion on what people may fear from *Transformation*, it's helpful to note that in most cases, change itself is not necessarily at the core of their anxiety. Although that may be a question of scale—what would seem to be reasonable change to one person might seem outlandish to another—most people accept the inevitability of change. Paraphrasing an old saying, the only thing that truly remains the same is change itself.

With that in mind, it can be helpful for leaders spearheading a major transition—not just one involving technology, but any sort of broad shift or reinvention—to redirect their attention to a different aspect of fear. This doesn't necessarily relate to anything specific, but rather touches on fear of loss. By experiencing change, many people fear that they will somehow lose something of value that simply can't be replaced by something else. For some, it may be a job. For others, a way of life, or "the way things used to be," whatever that may mean.

Here, it can be helpful to reinforce the varied benefits of digital transformation, from greater productivity to a more creative approach to work. In that sense, you're sharing the message that whatever someone may fear losing—be it something tangible or even something imaginary—thoughtful *Transformation* doesn't leave a void with nothing else stepping up to fill the space. It can be construed as loss, but what takes its place—if the *Transformation* proceeds smoothly and transparently—will be better than what's in the rearview mirror.

Another angle of fear of loss does, in fact, have to do with what change actually entails. For many, change promotes fear that they will fail to catch on to new ideas, mindsets, and processes—that somehow they'll be the only one in the group who simply can't adapt, learn, and leverage something that so many others are raving about.

Again, patience and thoughtful sharing of information are critical in addressing this very understandable concern. Substantial training and support can help even the most digital-phobic individual to relax—at least somewhat—about their ability to become comfortable with something that seems so distant and alien.

Citibank certainly learned that the hard way. Following a digital initiative, the bank accidentally sent around $900 million to lenders early, causing considerable financial damage to Citibank. The snafu was attributed to a software user interface that only confused employees and contractors alike. Citibank went to court to try to recover the money—and lost.[12]

Additionally, it's also useful to point out—repeatedly if necessary—that most people are in the same boat when it comes to understanding new ways of working. Many of us have little backgro und in, or familiarity with, everything that can go into a digitally driven *Transformation*. For the most part, we're all learning as we go—and an environment of mutual support and understanding can promote the confidence that often accompanies a solid sense of community and shared challenge.

REMEMBER, COMPLETE BUY-IN IS RARELY POSSIBLE—AT FIRST

Change is a scary proposition for many of us. It's unknown, the steps to achieve it can be difficult and time consuming, and the ultimate outcome—ideally a positive one—is rarely a certainty. So don't be shocked if, despite whatever steps you've taken to illustrate the mechanics as well as the benefits of *Transformation*, some in your organization are simply hesitant to embrace and support what you're trying to achieve. That said, it pays to be prepared should that very real possibility become a reality.

Step one is to avoid ostracizing those with this perspective. However compelling your argument has been, singling people out for their hesitancy or objections is, if nothing else, completely counterproductive. The attitude of, "If you're not with me, you're against me," never wins anybody over—at least in a genuine sense.

Begin by empathizing with those who are slow to buy in. And that means asking them to explain what about the initiative they disagree with or makes them feel uncomfortable.

Give them a forum for expressing their concerns or fears about what's changing. The mere fact that you're offering them a chance to speak and be heard can potentially begin to soften a teammate's reticence or fears.

While you should look to keep the discussion as empirical as possible, don't disregard beliefs, attitudes, or other factors that may contribute to their positions. To win them over, you'll have to address every aspect of their objections or hesitancy.

However illogical or even outrageous the reasons for hesitant buy-in may be, try to be as understanding as possible. Try not to take anything personally. Remember that it's possible to listen to someone thoughtfully without agreeing with a single word they might utter.

At this point, it can be helpful to reiterate your position and revisit some of the primary points and arguments in favor of the upcoming *Transformation*. Stress potential benefits, both individual and team-wide. Identify what elements of the initiative simply don't align with your teammate's worries or doubts. If possible, go point by point in touching on an individual's concerns and, from there, offer tangible evidence and counterarguments that mitigate them.

Unfortunately, here's where things can potentially become a bit dicey. Simply put, make it clear to anyone on the fence that being "sort of on board" won't contribute to the project's success and may, in fact, hinder it. That's not to say that everyone must be an out-and-out cheerleader ready to run through a brick wall out of passion for the cause.

But it is critical to expect a certain level of support. To offer hesitant colleagues the chance to adjust their positions and beliefs, make it clear what you will expect of them moving forward. Identify the attitudes and behaviors that will be acceptable and those that can't be tolerated for the good of the initiative or the organization. Setting what can be construed as a minimum standard of buy-in is a reasonable form of compromise and may, over time, move reticent employees toward positions of support and enthusiasm.

Still, that may not be enough for some team members who make it clear they just can't see things your way. In that case, it might be the time to begin arranging a comfortable transition—possibly out of the company completely. Tell your teammate that it's obvious that the envisioned "fit" simply isn't going to happen and that you're willing to work together to facilitate some sort of readjustment. Emphasize that, given the circumstances, it's likely not in the best interests of the employee or the company for things to remain the way they are. Both the *Transformation* and the employee's professional future are too valuable to compromise.

However comprehensive, the first step in the LIFTS progression—learn—isn't necessarily going to be flawless. There will likely be misunderstandings and objections, regardless of how compelling your efforts are. But the goal is to educate as completely as possible, listen to your team, and work toward a consistent unity of purpose and determination.

NEED TO KNOW:

- The first step in embarking on a successful *Transformation* is to educate everyone impacted as much as possible about the ramifications, benefits, and other aspects.

- Reemphasize that *Transformation* means more than technology. Talk about reasons for the initiative, any form of necessary culture change, and other outcomes.

- Stress the benefits of *Transformation* regarding individuals as well as the entire organization. Look for collaborative forms of benefit that take in more than just one group or individual.

- Take the time to understand why some teammates may be nervous about such significant change—or, for that matter, why they oppose it.

- Empathize with those holding out as much as you can, and work to help them better understand your support for *Transformation*. But make it clear that a "sorta support" attitude may not be sufficient and, as a result, might warrant an individual's consideration of moving on in a way that won't run counter to your transformative efforts.

CHAPTER 9

INVESTIGATE

SCHOOL'S OUT—TO A CERTAIN extent. The learning phase of the transformative process is, by now, largely behind you. That's not to say that a good deal of education doesn't await you and your team—after all, *Transformation* is an ongoing journey without any genuine set destination. But ideally at this point, you and your colleagues have a reasonably complete understanding of what *Transformation* in your organization entails—as well as how everyone will be impacted by it.

Now we're on to phase two—investigation. Before moving forward in any meaningful way, it's essential to gain a sense of where you are, what you and your company can bring to the situation, and any risks and potential pitfalls.

But the focus is not purely on foreseeable problems. Rather, this is a time characterized largely by potential and opportunity. By developing a comprehensive view of where you are and where you want to go, you can identify key areas—be they financial, functional, or social—where the most fertile points of opportunity can be found. That way, when elements of your *Transformation* begin to move into place, you'll have a clear sense of where to concentrate your energy and resources.

This is the second step in the overall LIFTS scheme—a systematic, easy-to-follow, and, above all, logical progression that effectively builds toward the point where you're in the best position possible to put all the tools and planning into practice.

This can be a challenging point, as there are many issues and factors to consider. To help you along, I've included several systems arranged around acronyms to help you choose—and use—those strategies that can help you find out all you need to know.

Keeping matters as simple and straightforward as possible, the investigation stage really boils down to three basic components:

- *Organization*: What organizational structure exists that can impact your planned *Transformation*—and are you ready for the *Transformation* itself?

- *External*: Which outside forces may also influence *Transformation*?

- *Risk*: What are the significant changes in technology that have broadened the focus of risk management from the micro-project view to a much wider perspective?

These three elements encapsulate the investigation phase. By taking all three into sufficient account, you're preparing your organization as completely as possible to begin the actual implementation of *Transformation* with genuine confidence in both your own capabilities and what you'll likely need to address moving forward. That's where the magic of *Transformation* truly begins to take hold.

ORGANIZATION—ARE YOU READY?

Three significant forces influence how business and technology executives think about organization structures for managing technology today:[1]

- *Demand forces fuel the need for rapid, innovative, safe, and cost-effective use of technology.* With technology increasingly embedded into products, services, business processes, and relationships, firms must constantly nurture creative and innovative uses. A firm must also encourage initiatives for technology-based competitive maneuvering, productivity, and cost leveraging. Managing these demands requires the blending of business and technology knowledge. When only business executives possess insights about business opportunities and needs—and only technology executives are savvy about how information technologies might support or shape business opportunities—the situation is neither optimal nor sustainable. Instead, demand pressures require organizational structures that facilitate collaboration among business and technology executives so that they can innovate and experiment.

- *Supply forces require delivery of reliable and cost-effective technology.* With the horizontal fragmentation of technology and the viability of outsourcing and offshoring options, it is hard to find a firm that doesn't cite "solutions integration" as a major path to added value. That means managing relationships with a diverse number of service providers. It also means rapid delivery of applications by fast-cycle projects and maintaining a workforce with crucial competencies in technology skills. Well-designed organizational structures can deliver effective management of external partnerships and human capital. Strategic sourcing and the ability to manage relationships with a diverse number of service providers through multi-sourcing agreements is critical.

- *Administrative forces require better technology management.* Almost everywhere today, technology assets are a significant proportion of the capital base—often in excess of 50 percent. This carries a range of administrative imperatives: greater oversight and management of technology productivity and risk; appropriate controls and audits as an integral element of enterprise risk management; and continual benchmarking of technology costs, with transparent costing models for services. Organizational models must explicitly enable the financial management and control of technology. Similarly, strategic planning for technology must direct attention toward the timing of investments, anticipating emerging business needs and developing appropriate infrastructure and ability to deliver services. Organizational models must ensure that this strategic planning is carried out with verifiable results, rather than sitting on a shelf.

- *Nurture relationship networks for visioning, innovation, and sourcing.* This model emphasizes the importance of four stakeholder categories: the board and top management, business management, technology management, and external vendors. Three kinds of important relationship networks exist with regard to these groups: visioning, innovation, and sourcing.

Visioning networks involve senior business and technology executives, as well as the board. This fosters collaboration for creating and articulating a strategic vision about the role and value of technology. Visioning networks help top management teams describe their perspectives on the role of technology, their strategic priorities for its use, and the links they see between it and drivers of business strategy. One of the mechanisms for establishing a visioning network is to have the chief information officer (CIO) or chief digital officer (CDO) as a formal member of the top management team. Other strategies include the establishment of a Technology Management Council and a Technology Investment Board.

Innovation networks involve business and technology executives. They foster collaboration for conceptualizing and implementing technology applications. These applications are often aimed at enhancing the firm's agility and innovation in customer relationships, manufacturing, product development, supply chain management or enterprise control, and

NETWORKED GOVERNANCE MODEL

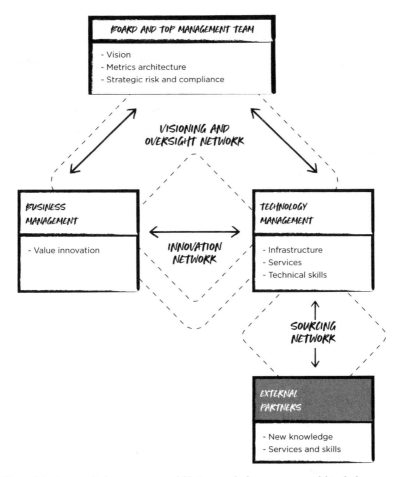

Figure 9.1. A networked governance model.² A networked governance model includes a visioning and oversight network, an innovation network, and a sourcing network.

governance systems. One example of organizational mechanisms that promote innovation networks is a corporate and divisional project approval committee. Whereas visioning networks engage the board and the top management to shape overall perspectives about the strategic role and value of technology, innovation networks focus on specific innovations and strategic applications.

Sourcing networks are relationship networks between technology executives and external partners. Their purpose is to foster collaboration between these internal and external parties when they are negotiating and managing multi-sourcing arrangements, joint ventures, or strategic alliances. Sourcing networks can help companies not only lower their costs but also augment their capabilities and thinking about innovative uses of technology. Attention to sourcing networks must be emphasized in key organizational units that deal with the technical architecture and infrastructure (for example, the Office of Architecture and Standards) and the management of technology investments, such as the Enterprise Program Management Office (EPMO).

Organize to Manage Three Categories

Successful implementation of technology management capabilities requires not only the design of effective organizational structures but also the attention to three categories of processes: *foundation*, *primary*, and *secondary* (see Figure 9.2).

Foundation processes are aimed at managing supply pressures and connecting with infrastructure and human capital.

Primary processes are aimed at managing demand pressures and relate to the delivery and support of business capabilities through enabling technology and services. Broken down further, there are three primary processes:

- *Value innovation*: Conceptualizing strategic technology needs and opportunities in the form of applications

- *Solutions delivery*: Building technology applications

- *Services provisioning*: Providing help desk, desktop configuration, and other support services

PROCESS CATEGORIES

FOUNDATION PROCESSES FOR SUPPLY-SIDE MANAGEMENT	
Infrastructure management	Activities for building and managing the architectural blueprint for investments in computing, networking, database, object-base, and other key information technologies to deliver a range of communication, collaboration, and productivity-enhancing tools and services. Includes the establishment and management of infrastructure standards.
Human capital management	Acquiring, developing, and retaining talent with an emphasis on managing the portfolio of technology skills needed today and in the future.

PRIMARY PROCESSES FOR DEMAND-SIDE MANAGEMENT	
Value innovation	Strategic analysis of business opportunities for the use of technology and conceptualization of ways in which it can be used to strengthen business competencies, customer relationships, or partner networks. Developing the business case and investment rationale for the strategic applications and establishing the value metrics.
Solutions delivery	Delivering applications either through internal development, external contracting, or solutions integration of packaged software.
Services provisioning	The provisioning of utilities, such as data center, and services, such as helpdesk and desktop management, for users across the corporation.

SECONDARY PROCESSES FOR ADMINISTRATIVE MANAGEMENT	
Technology strategic planning	Activities aimed at managing the key issues of supply and demand for technology. These issues include the screening of emerging information technologies, technology infrastructure and services planning, human capital planning, and applications portfolio planning.
Technology financial management	Activities associated with financial management and control, auditing, and risk management. Examples of these activities include the structuring of service level agreements, tracking and benchmarking the cost of services, developing the business case and ROI analyses of infrastructure investment proposals, developing value scorecards for projects, and supporting the monitoring of risks and detection of fraud.

Figure 9.2. Process categories.[3] *Three categories of processes must be addressed by an organizational structure.*

These processes are the touch points through which business clients perceive and appreciate the quality, contributions, and effectiveness of technology.

Secondary processes are related to administrative needs and requirements. Their contribution is measured by how well they support and enable the foundation and primary processes. The two secondary processes are strategic planning and financial management.

MANAGING EXTERNAL FACTORS

Let's shift our attention to means with which you can study potential external factors. One that's specific to outside influence goes by the acronym PESTLE.

I am a very big fan of PESTLE. The system was invented more than fifty years ago by Francis Aguilar, an American scholar who specialized in strategic planning. In the late 1960s, Aguilar published *Scanning the Business Environment*, a book in which he introduced the concept of PESTLE.[4]

If you're not familiar with the term, PESTLE refers to six areas where it's essential to understand critical factors in your environment that impact you and your company:

- Political
- Economic
- Social
- Technological
- Legal
- Environmental

A core element of successful application of the PESTLE system is posing a series of questions about the potential influence and impact of those six areas. In so doing, you're able to compile a comprehensive breakdown that can indicate not only potential problems and challenges but also specific areas of leverage and opportunity. Knowing that, you can then, in effect, personalize aspects and features of your planned *Transformation* to reflect both reality and opportunity.

Let's take a closer look at the six PESTLE components.

Political

This first area takes in both the potential impact of government and the influence of various political factors. With regard to government, what actions, policies, or legislation may affect your particular industry or the economy as a whole? When building your analysis in this sector, consider such elements as taxes, fiscal policies, tariffs, legislation impacting competition and transparency, and other issues. Depending on the setting, topics such as political stability, or lack thereof, may also play a significant role in your organization's activities and prospects.

Economic

How well is the economy as a whole performing? What's trending? For instance, if inflation is an issue, that will impact your pricing of services and products, as well as consumers' ability to afford them. Additionally, the interchange between this area and government is important—what's the government doing to combat inflation? Other factors to consider include interest rate trends, movement in the stock market, foreign currency exchange rates, and other financially related patterns and actions.

Social

This area cuts across a variety of factors—some rather empirical, others less so. One example of the former is demographics—how is the composition of your market changing regarding the age, ethnicity, finances, and other components of the market or markets you address? Cultural trends are also a primary component, such as shopping for special holidays and other time-specific events and celebrations.

Technological

Of particular value to a *Transformation* that includes a digital ingredient, this sector focuses specifically on technology and how changes and innovations may affect your organization, industry, and community. Taking in research, development, automation, and more current topics such as machine learning and AI, technological assessment also considers technological growth and maturity. How technically current are you and your industry as a whole? Given the exponential growth and evolution of technology, this is a particularly important consideration when assessing just where you are and where you wish to go through *Transformation*.

Legal

The multifaceted issue of the law considers both external and internal elements. From the outside are laws and regulations imposed by governmental and regulatory bodies—yet another crossover with the political area. Additionally, there are the rules and regulations that you and your organization choose to follow of your own accord—internal policies, procedures, and rules of the road that you develop internally. Laws on both the inside and outside take in consumer law, safety parameters and standards, labor law, and other issues. Another crossover area connects legal with social considerations. In effect, are you and your organization good citizens? Do you follow the letter of the law and, ideally, go further by establishing internal standards that further boost compliance and good practices?

Environmental

This final area shares many aspects with its five prior brethren. On the one hand, there's a social connection, particularly with regard to environmental issues. Does your organization stand out as a champion for the environment? Legally speaking, is your compliance sufficient? Additional considerations can depend on your industry. For instance, tourism is impacted by climate and weather. Certain forms of manufacturing have to consider issues such as pollution and climate change. Once more, is your organization in line with externally established standards and rules, or do you take things further of your own accord?

As you can tell by now, the PESTLE approach to evaluating various possible sources of impact on your company and planned *Transformation* is decidedly comprehensive. Done properly, it affords you a thorough overview of many factors that can influence not only your organizational reinvention but also, moving forward, how to leverage that change to optimize your goals and objectives.

Ultimately, that comes down to how well you service the people most central to your business—your customers. That suggests an equally comprehensive dive into the heart of that group—your target market.

KNOWING YOUR TARGET MARKET

With the involved planning, information gathering, and other steps leading toward a transformative initiative, raising the issue of a target market might seem like a needless backslide into Business 101. At this point in your company's growth and maturation, revisiting what's usually considered as basic a step as knowing to whom you're targeting your efforts can feel rather silly.

It's not in the least. For one thing, any organization with some history behind it always does well to revisit its understanding of what it believes its target market to be. You've likely changed, and so have your optimal markets. Making sure you're still connecting in the way you want to is both sensible and forward thinking.

That's particularly true about *Transformation*. By pursuing a significant recrafting of how you operate—particularly with a digital role—you're potentially positioning your company to address a decidedly different target market than any you may have focused on before. While that market may present far greater opportunity for explosive growth, you may well have to approach it in a different manner.

So, take the time to have another look at your target market. Using segmentation not entirely different from that employed in the PESTLE methodology, consider various elements that can impact who composes that particular sweet spot:

- *Geographic segmentation*: Where are your customers located? Are there particular "hot spots" where your market is especially concentrated, or does physical location have little to do with the people you serve? Consider the impact of digital transformation—will that effectively change or expand where you will conduct business and with whom?

- *Demographic and socioeconomic segmentation*: This can prove something of a moving target subject to constant change, but consider the following characteristics of individuals who compose your target market:

  ○ *Gender*: Who likes what you do—males, females, people who are transgender, non-binary, non-conforming? Does some or all of what you offer appeal to all groups equally? Further, does digital transformation offer an opportunity to readjust the gender mix to your advantage?

  ○ *Age*: Baby Boomers, Millennials, Gen X, or Gen Z—is there any sort of particular concentration of age?

  ○ *Income level*: Do your products and services appeal more to affluent consumers, or is your market broader?

  ○ *Occupation*: Does work matter?

  ○ *Education*: Do you appeal to more educated people, or is education largely irrelevant?

○ *Household size*: This factor can closely correlate with many of the parameters cited previously. Is your customer base composed of large families, or do you hold more appeal to single buyers?

○ *Stage in family life cycle*: If your market is made up of families, where are most of them along the continuum? Do you look toward younger, perhaps smaller families, households with teens, or empty nesters?

• *Attitudes*: This can prove very useful in further delineating the makeup of your target market. Although information such as demographics is undeniably important in understanding your market, two people with similar backgrounds and other demographic factors in common may, in fact, think and feel quite differently. Digging beneath the surface a bit further involves considering how individuals approach things in a different manner. Consider the following:

○ *Motivation*: What gets people pumped up and excited?

○ *Opinions*: What do they think of certain ideas, issues, and other points of consideration?

○ *Purchase priorities*: What matters most when they're making buying decisions?

○ *Brand evaluation*: How happy do they tend to be with their buying decisions? Further, what do they associate with different types of brands?

○ *Alignment*: What do they strongly agree with? What do they absolutely oppose or object to?

• *Psychological profile*: Also known as *psychographics*, psychological profiles are similar to data regarding attitude but focus more on psychological characteristics and traits such as values, desires, goals, interests, and lifestyle choices. For instance, is a good portion of your target market extroverts or introverts? Are they religious? What are their personal and professional interests? Incorporating this information into your target market research can add an additional layer of insight, suggesting how to adjust your products and services to better sync with your customers, as well as what marketing you can employ to connect with them effectively.

These and other similar questions allow you to peel away at the onion that is your target market, allowing you to gain a more comprehensive and useful understanding of what makes your target audience tick.

A DIFFERENT PERSPECTIVE—TARGET MARKET SIZE AND GROWTH

Having a comprehensive understanding of the components and characteristics of your target market is essential when assessing your current status, as well as the potential impact of significant *Transformation*. It can be every bit as helpful to employ a different breakdown when determining not only who's in your target market but also who you can effectively reach.

A simplified view is depicted in Figure 9.3. Business strategists discover profitable opportunities—new market spaces or gaps in existing market spaces—by considering the following: signals regarding product/service, customer, technology, socioeconomic, and cultural trends; competitors' current and future strategic positions; the organization's internal competencies; and recognition of the competencies it might gain access to through partners.[5]

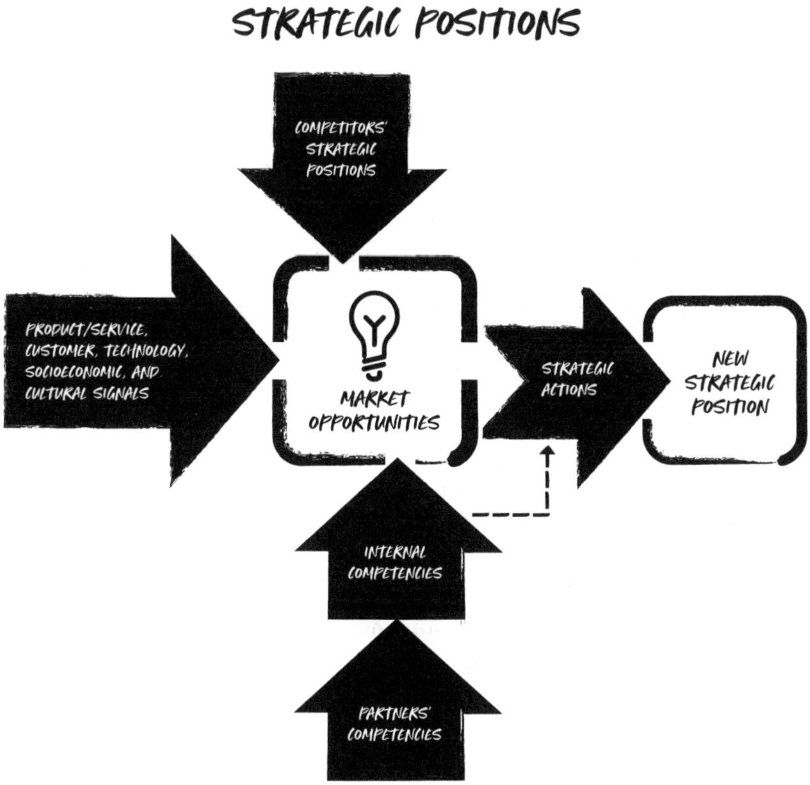

STRATEGIC POSITIONS

Figure 9.3. Establishing strategic positions.[6] Companies discover market opportunities by considering internal competencies and external signals.

This particular exercise begins by identifying your *total available market*. Also referred to as *total addressable market*, this is the overall revenue opportunity that is available to a product or service if 100 percent market share is achieved.

The most reliable way to calculate total available market is by running what's called a bottom-up analysis of an industry. This involves tallying the total number of customers in a market and multiplying that number by the average annual revenue of each customer.

Obviously, being able to bat a thousand with regard to the entirety of your market is utterly unrealistic. Accordingly, you can begin to pare that back toward a more viable target. This is referred to as your *serviceable available market*. A serviceable available market allows businesses to objectively estimate the portion of the market they can realistically acquire—needless to say, far more attainable than the proverbial entire smash.

You can calculate your serviceable available market by adding up all the potential customers that would be a good fit for your business. From there, multiply that by the average annual revenue of these types of customers.

Now you can plug in a step that, if you've been working alongside my suggested chronology, you've already completed. Match up what you've determined when narrowing the potential market with the characteristics of your actual target market—demographic information, attitudes, psychological profiles, and other elements of your core market objective. This takes the winnowing process even further to correlate just the sort of customers who are verifiably in your wheelhouse.

Now for the final step in this exercise—your actual market share. This is your foothold, so to speak, in the overall marketplace universe—your slice of the pie. The calculation is relatively straightforward. Starting with a customer's total purchases of a product or service, what percentage goes to your company? For instance, if a group of consumers buys 100 bottles of dish detergent, and you're in the fortunate position of selling 40 of those, you hold a 40-percent market share. (There's also a market share based more on value than volume.)

Market share is understandably significant in several ways. For one thing, it's an empirical measure of consumers' preference for one product over others. That breaks down further to greater sales achieved more efficiently, as well as more solid barriers to limit competitor entry. Even better, a higher market share also means that if the market expands, the leader stands to gain more than the others.

But that enviable status carries a caveat. Even as a market leader exerts its dominance, it also has to expand the market to achieve additional growth. Simply put, a bigger slice of the pie mandates a larger pie—and you've got to do much of the baking. And gaining a useful view of just what that might entail involves an additional process that pinpoints other potential sources of impact on growth. One way to do that is to employ Porter's Five Forces.

PORTER'S FIVE FORCES

Named after Harvard Business School professor Michael Porter, Porter's Five Forces is a model that defines and breaks down five competitive forces that shape every industry.[7] In so doing, it measures an industry's resilience, weaknesses, strengths, and other elements. The system is useful to better understand the makeup of an industry to help craft corporate strategy— and, for us, it's a terrific way to further round out your investigation of external forces. Following are the five forces:

- *Industry competition*: The first force takes in the number of companies in a particular sector and gauges their capacity to make a dent in the performance of competitors. Not surprisingly, the greater the number of competitors, the less the influence any one player has. By contrast, the fewer the rivals, the better companies and industry leaders in particular are positioned to leverage prices and other factors to boost revenue.

- *Possible new entrants*: Following up on the issue of competition, the next force—logically enough—covers industry newcomers. The more quickly and profitably a new entrant can gain a foothold, the greater the threat to other more established competitors. Technological growth and maturation have emboldened this area—armed with just an app and energy, a newcomer can make a serious dent much faster than their predecessors whose entry was often more constrained and deliberate.

- *Influence of suppliers*: Here, the capacity of suppliers to tinker with the cost of supplies is addressed. Once again, a head count matters. The greater the number of given suppliers, the greater the options a company has to switch to another less costly supplier, if need be. But the smaller the number of suppliers, the greater the influence any one has on pricing and other costs.

- *Influence of customers*: The same dynamic that applies to suppliers also holds true regarding consumers. The greater the number of customers—or, additionally, the greater the number of customers with relatively modest buying activity—the less impact they can have on prices. But if a company has relatively few buyers or has customers who spend a great deal of money, those customers can bring more influence to bear on prices—generally through negotiation.

- *The possibility of substitutes*: Anything that can be used as a viable substitute for an existing product or service represents an additional force. While companies with relatively few, if any, competitors producing cheaper wares are at an advantage, those having to deal with less expensive replacements are far more vulnerable.

Taken together, Porter's Five Forces can prove invaluable in delineating strategy and use of resources. Overall, it can provide a comprehensive picture of an industry's overall attractiveness and potential for profitability and growth. Specific to digital technology, the influence of Porter's Five Forces is particularly acute. For instance, digitalization makes entry of new competitors theoretically more viable. On the other side of the coin, *Transformation* with a digital component can also benefit existing players, such as a company that implements a digital framework and, as a result, is better able to manage and negotiate with suppliers, as well as fend off aggressive, competitive newbies.

To better assess your current situation and make smarter decisions as a result, break down Porter's forces a bit further to identify significant components. For instance, with competition, identify key national competitors as well as prominent international competitors. From there, pinpoint potential sources of substitutes, as well as new possible industry entrants.

Be as thorough as possible with specific elements relating to each factor, including revenue, profit, market share, primary focus of activities, number of employees, product quality, and any other characteristics you consider significant. The more detail you have at hand, the better the level of your competitor assessment will be.

JUST SWOT IT

To augment the discussion of external threats, a suggested methodology that can be used in conjunction with external threat is *SWOT*.

SWOT stands for *strengths, weaknesses, opportunities,* and *threats.* SWOT allows you to analyze what your company currently does best and those areas that could stand for improvement.

Further, SWOT also considers potential points of vulnerability that competitors could leverage if you don't do something first to mitigate the threat.

Overall, SWOT encompasses an assessment of what's going on inside your business. Particular to the methodology included in this chapter so far, it also allows you to bring together much of the data you've already compiled into a thorough and synergistic analysis, letting you see not only all the elements that may be involved but also their relationship to one another.

Compiling a SWOT analysis isn't particularly difficult. But once again, the most effective SWOT analysis derives from as detailed and thorough a collection of information as possible, as well as a frank, pull-no-punches approach. It's imperative that you approach both the good and the bad with absolute candor. That, in turn, will offer the clearest picture of strategy moving forward.

- *Strengths*: These are the things your organization does particularly well. Alternatively, these can also be strengths that serve to separate you from competitors. This can range from the talent and motivation of your teammates to established, affordable relationships with suppliers. Don't overlook the role of a strong culture here, particularly one that's evolving or has already moved toward a mindset and values that support significant *Transformation*.

- *Weaknesses*: This is the category that includes issues that aren't exactly world-beaters. The same components that could potentially come across as advantages can, given the right circumstances, slip into weaknesses, such as stability of employee retention, use of resources, and other elements. Consider as well how those on the outside perceive your organization. What might they consider a weakness?

- *Opportunities*: This is already covered in various capacities so far, but it is nonetheless an important element of the SWOT matrix. In simple terms, what can you leverage or exploit moving forward? What might change that could open up opportunity that doesn't exist yet (such as changes in legislation or demographic shifts that impact your target audience)?

- *Threats*: What might have a negative effect on your current state, as well as your future? Again, reexamine the list of factors included in this chapter—can any of them be construed as a genuine problem on the horizon?

SWOT methodology is designed to afford you a detailed, comprehensive view of factors that could potentially impact your planned

Transformation. Additionally, you'll notice that certain elements of SWOT—such as opportunities and threats—slide over to address external factors as well, echoing the previous chapter's discussion on business strategy and technology investments.

THE RISKS ARE THERE— DO SOMETHING ABOUT THEM

Lastly, we come to the third area of the investigation phase—risk.

Let's get one thing out of the way. Anyone who suggests that sweeping *Transformation* isn't a dicey proposition is either completely naive or completely dishonest.

Some of these risks include the following:[8]

- *Business model risk* refers to the robustness of the business model and how well it is being executed.

- *Competitive risk* refers to the ability to sustain competitive action and retaliation.

- *Investment risk* is the ability to manage technology spending in a business environment where capital is scarce and technologies are volatile, expensive, and not easily understood.

- *Integration risk* covers the risks of inadequate integration between technology investments and business processes.

- *Misalignment risk* refers to inadequate alignment between technology spending and business priorities.

- *Governance models risk* addresses the risks of inadequate participation and involvement of cross-functional executives on key strategic and management decisions.

STRATEGIC RISKS

STRATEGIC RISK	DESCRIPTION

Business model risk	- How robust is the current business model?
	- What are the threats to the execution of the current business model due to:
	  · Premature technology?
	  · Poor training of employees?
	  · Failure to understand the motivations of customers and business partners?
	  · Poor project implementation?

Competitive risk	- How alert are we to opportunities for technology-based innovation? - Can competitors strategically outmaneuver us with innovative digital products, services, or business models? - Are our digital business models sustainable?

Investment risk	From a technology perspective:
	  - Are we spending the right amount?
	  - Are we spending on the right types, and is our timing right?
	  - Are our investment strategies appropriate to their organizational roles?
	  - Are we alert to emerging trends?

Integration risk	- How well are our business processes integrated and enabled with technology?

Misalignment risk	From a technology perspective:
	  - Do investments address business priorities?
	  - Do business executives adhere to existing standards for acquisition?
	  - Are data ownership and management policies clearly articulated and understood?

Technology governance models risk	- Do business executives champion strategic technology initiatives? - Is the business case for technology articulated through the corporate metrics hierarchy? - How well does technology collaborate in developing strategic initiatives?

Figure 9.4. Strategic risks.[9] Several categories of strategic risks must be managed.

The past three decades of business computing have contributed much to our understanding of risk regarding technology. Unfortunately, this work has been rather narrow, focused on controlling and managing projects rather than on the broader risks that executives face in firms where technology is deeply and fundamentally embedded within the business. Indeed, the turn of the century has heralded significant changes in the technology milieu that have created a compelling need to expand the focus of risk management from the micro-project view to a broader enterprise perspective.

These changes include an increasing emphasis on buying and customizing packaged solutions rather than building systems in-house (that is, on solutions integration rather than software development); partnering with a wide array of providers to acquire needed technical competencies and skills, including taking advantage of offshore resources; using technology for systems that span organizational boundaries and help link customers by leveraging electronic commerce and CRM systems; and deploying technology as the platform on which the entire business is run.

THE NATURE OF TECHNOLOGY RISK

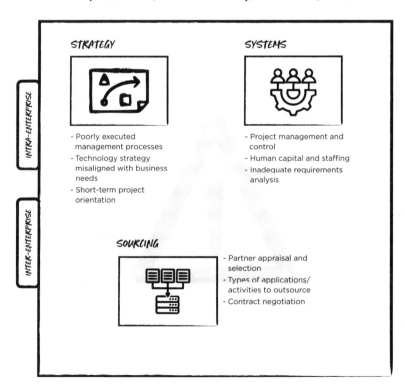

Figure 9.5. The nature of technology risk. Risks can be categorized in strategy, systems, and sourcing categories.

In this environment where technology is pervasive, what is the nature of risk? In Figure 9.5, these risks are classified into three broad categories: strategy, systems, and sourcing, based on where they originate. Some risks are predominantly intra-enterprise in nature, such as systems and strategy, whereas others, notably sourcing, reflect the challenges that arise in interorganizational settings. Note that although these categories are somewhat overlapping and not mutually exclusive, they nonetheless provide a conceptually simple framework that can be developed and maintained through conversations and interactions among executives from both technology and business.

Risks originating from systems are typically intraorganizational, although in some instances when external partners are used for system development and integration, they may be interorganizational in nature. The risks derive from all aspects of systems deployment, including project planning and control; human capital and staffing; inadequate user requirements; changes in technology; the complexity, scope, and structure of systems; and inadequate support from senior management.

Managing Project Risk Is Becoming More Dynamic

The landscape for technology project management today is characterized by a strange paradox. On the one hand, very few firms develop large, multiyear software applications in-house, as was the practice in the past. Rather, they seek to leverage the speed with which packaged applications can be acquired and implemented. Thus, the typical project involves system integration rather than system development. On the other hand, the growing complexity and scope of today's enterprise applications often result in implementations that last for only two to three years. These applications typically necessitate significant changes to business processes, reporting relationships, and decision-making structures, thereby contributing to further lengthening of the implementation cycle. Yet, competitive pressures and increasing business velocity demand that application provisioning be accomplished in a speedy manner.

Additionally, service providers and vendors are increasingly used to assist in system integration, leading to project teams composed of a mix of internal employees and multiple external partners. All these factors collectively create an extremely dynamic and complex project management environment. That can go a long way toward combating the high failure rate that many technology projects experience.

What are the risks embedded in such fast-cycle, multifunctional projects? For the past two decades, scholars have examined the major sources of risk in technology projects. In Figure 9.6, based on a recent synthesis of this research, project risks are summarized into six major categories: organizational environment, user, requirements, project complexity, planning and control, and team.

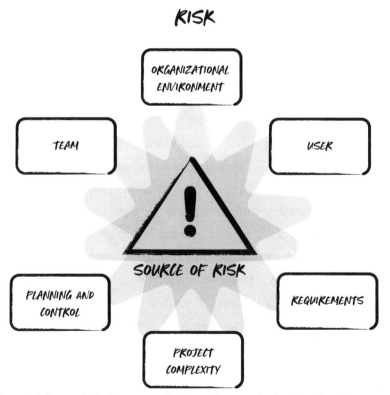

Figure 9.6. Source of risk. There are six fundamental sources of risk to be addressed in managing business and technology.

The organizational environment refers to the broader context within which the target system will be integrated and implemented. Frequently, culture, politics, other concurrent change initiatives, and the support of top management affect the likelihood of project success. In general, when the culture is not open to technological change, where vested interests have different perspectives on the importance of the system, where there are other significant organizational changes occurring, and where top management does not send strong signals endorsing the project, environments have been found to be riskier.

Systems are developed for use by organizational personnel to accomplish operational, strategic, and tactical goals. Not surprisingly, user involvement in every phase of the project is critical for success. User risk occurs when users are "disenfranchised" and their input is not sought in every aspect of system conceptualization, selection, design, and customization.

Research has consistently shown that in situations where users are not involved, negative attitudes are formed, ultimately leading to implementation failure.

A related risk is the peril of inadequate requirements determination—in plain language, users don't clearly express what they need. Ambiguous or poorly stated requirements lead to systems and processes that are poorly matched with users' desires and are often relegated to the technology no-man's-land called *shelfware*. Performing a thorough and complete requirements analysis helps ensure that the outcomes of the project are aligned with users' goals (for example, performance improvements, better information, speedier transactions) and increase their willingness to accept and use the system.

Projects can be seen in the context of complexity. In general, more complex projects are also riskier. Project complexity is an outcome of several factors, including the newness of the technology, the number and complexity of the business processes and applications involved, and the number of organizational units and individuals who are likely to be affected by the project.

Planning and control risks can occur in the typical project management activities associated with any complex project. These include risks related to developing project schedule and milestones, monitoring project progress, and estimating resource requirements.

Arguably, project management is one of the most important capabilities an organization needs to possess—regardless of the scope and size of its operations. An inability to successfully execute any of these activities increases the likelihood of failure. Even if a new system is eventually delivered "successfully," inadequate attention to planning and control risks often results in schedule and budget overruns and reduces the overall value of the project.

Finally, team risk reflects the people element of projects. Project teams are generally composed of members from a wide variety of backgrounds and functional areas and may include professionals from partner organizations as well. Accordingly, the first challenge arises in assembling the right mix and level of skills and knowledge to accomplish the project. Here, consider implementing enterprise resource planning project teams—people charged with knowing just how technology can best be used. Not only do such teams need to understand the nuances of the software, but they also have to possess a deep understanding of the business processes that will be affected by the software.

A second major challenge is communication barriers between technology professionals and users and between internal employees and external consultants. Developing the right *esprit de corps* in the team is a key prerequisite for system success.

It's important to note that the risk categories described here affect each other and interact in multiple and sometimes unanticipated ways. For instance, requirements risk and user risk are interrelated. To the extent that the organizational environment is unstable because of current business imperatives, organizational environment risk contributes to requirements risk. Likewise, project complexity risk and team risk are related—the more complex the project, the greater the requirement for high levels of knowledge and skills, and, therefore, the possibility for higher team risk is amplified.

Finally, most types of project risks are amplified when projects span large geographical distances, time zones, and cultures, as in the case of projects involving offshore sources. Effectively managing project risk requires that a structured process and organizational responsibilities be implemented at both the project and program levels.

A formal risk management plan should be developed to clarify risk management roles and responsibilities; risk management processes, procedures, standards, training, and tools; the method and frequency of risk progress reporting; and what should be monitored to determine whether risks actually exist. A project should attempt to manage only the risks it can handle. Other risks should be elevated to the program level. The decision of whether to make this shift should be made based on examination of whether the mitigation action steps are within the control of the project team.

Managing risk at a program level involves a review of project risks and program risks by an Enterprise Program Management Office (EPMO). The EPMO should analyze project risk across the entire program to determine whether the same risk occurs in different projects and requires concerted action. The EPMO should document the inventory of risks, as well as their assessment and mitigation plans, in a database. If, after analyzing program risk, the overall program risk level is deemed higher than originally documented in the cost/benefit plan (that is, the business case), the business case should be updated, reflecting the adjustment in the range of costs and/or benefits or a lower confidence measure. It is important that the EPMO collaborate with an enterprise risk management group to ensure that the business impacts of project-related risks are well understood and that periodic evaluation can be made concerning the impact of other enterprise risks on the project.

NEED TO KNOW:

- Develop strong partnerships between technology and users. Increase levels of trust and understanding by providing forums for frequent interactions. Strong partnerships promote user involvement, permit requirements to be defined in a more cooperative climate, ensure that technology investments are aligned with business priorities, and boost overall sense of ownership.

- Educate executives and knowledge workers about the unique challenges of technology. In many firms, users have a limited understanding of the complex technologies and the effort required to implement complex systems. As a result, their expectations are not realistic.

- Craft a comprehensive sourcing strategy that articulates the desired mix of insourcing, domestic outsourcing, and off-shoring—and further recognizes the long-term capability necessary to meet strategic objectives. A technology organization that's too lean and is also highly outsourced may inhibit the development of strategic applications, while too large an organization may not deliver desired business value in a cost-effective manner.

- Develop vendor management expertise that includes knowledge about location constraints, vendor performance, and vendor abilities. Such capabilities will facilitate careful vendor selection and help mitigate the multiple risks associated with outsourcing. Using pilot projects related to non-mission-critical applications is a low-risk tactic for learning the strengths and weaknesses of offshore locations.

- Instill a project management culture and imbue the technology organization with project management expertise.

continued

Project management is both a science and an art and needs to be formally learned and practiced on the job. Poor project management is one of the most significant risks that technology organizations face and can frequently spell the difference between firms that are able to exploit technology for business value and those that are not.

- Organize and manage based on value-creating processes. Do not set up committees for their own sake. Take stock of value-creating processes that these organizational structures will support. Remember that the level of complexity associated with an organizational unit will vary based on the sophistication of the governance network it supports. Apply a modular-organizing logic in designing critical technology organization structures. Consider explicitly assigning individual executives to each one of these modular organizational units.

- Recognize that organization design and change management are critical organizational capabilities. Organization design changes must be managed with care. Strong relationships need to be built with stakeholders. How can you promote "straight talk" in an environment that values commitment and relationships? How can you lead your team to accept that difficulties along the way are not failures, but rather a normal part of the change process? How will you resolve these rough spots and build on them to fuel the organizational change effort? Develop bottom-up change agents—rarely does change result solely from a top-down edict. Lower-level employees must buy in. Cultivating change agents can guarantee their support in selling their peers.

- Develop your communication strategy and management capability, which has significant implications for evolving organization structures. Therefore, communications strategy and management is the responsibility of the entire senior management team. They should be supported by expert communications professionals to ensure that the strategy is based on user feedback and goals; to define a path to move target audiences from mere awareness to understanding, commitment, and action; and to ensure that suitable research, timelines, and measurements of success are included.

CHAPTER 10

FORMULATE

SO FAR, THE PROCESS of moving toward a transformative initiative that will reinvent your organization has been largely preparatory in nature. That's not merely solid thinking; it's crucial to ensure the most successful outcome possible. It's the creation of essential capabilities that will allow you to create a path forward for your journey.

But the planning isn't quite done yet—nor is the process of narrowing and sharpening your focus to target those areas that offer the greatest possible potential.

So, it's time to formulate, the step in which, having performed extensive assessment, you can begin selecting those objectives that you've determined to mean the most to your organization—those that are aligned with what you are and what you aspire to be and are adequately supported by technology, governance, and processes. Further, from there, it will be important to effectively communicate those goals to everyone impacted by the initiative, ensuring not only their understanding of the ramifications of all that's happening but also their recognition of what they can specifically contribute.

That way, everyone has a hand in pulling the rope that will move your organization toward the transformed state you need it to become.

PORTFOLIO AND PROGRAM MANAGEMENT (PPM) ELEVATES DECISION-MAKING

This procedure is basic, known to anyone hoping to make sense of hundreds of songs or photos on a hard drive or wanting to clean out the basement: discover what you have, sort it into logical piles, and assess the value of the individual items against some larger goal.

In business, this procedure received a fancy name—portfolio management—but it is still elemental. In fact, its power is such that it might even be deemed critical. Managers of financial assets would not presume to act without it. It is widely applied in other management functions, including strategic planning and new product development. Most technology executives know of it, and many practice some form of it, but it has not often been granted the strategic role it deserves.

Many companies don't use this as extensively as they could because they see it only in financial terms—or they think of it as a software tool or just a tactical approach for managing projects. At its best, however, portfolio management as advanced by portfolio and program management (PPM) takes all of an organization's assets and activities into account. It is a way of doing business that gives the entire enterprise, from the boardroom down, better information to develop strategies, manage risk, and execute more effectively.

PPM is the enterprise-wide focus on defining, gathering, categorizing, analyzing, and monitoring information on corporate assets and activity. It provides top managers a centralized and balanced view of the payoffs of various projects while also highlighting benefits and risks.[1]

An effective PPM approach can unite an organization's efforts at every level. It is a completely different way of seeing, assessing, and planning the business—analogous, to a degree, to financial portfolio management. For example, in finance, where the concept of portfolio management originated, an investor identifies and categorizes all assets and collects them in a portfolio. This allows the investor to see various aggregated views of individual investments. The investor might notice, for instance, that the portfolio is weighted too heavily in one industry, has redundant exposure to one type of security, or carries a certain level of risk or return. The investor can then set a strategy and construct a portfolio likely to achieve an appropriate balance of risk-return.

In much the same way, digital asset portfolios reveal what a company owns. Technology project portfolios can reveal what its various branches are trying to accomplish. From there, it can decide which pieces of all this activity are more likely to support the enterprise business strategy.

PPM PLAYS A STRATEGIC ROLE

Effective PPM can help a company better align technology spending with current and future business needs. PPM creates information and insight to help executives and managers make a variety of decisions:

- Defining business improvement options and scenarios
- Analyzing implications and impact of potential initiatives
- Setting target allocations for investment categories
- Evaluating and making decisions on project requests
- Evaluating the health of digital assets
- Determining appropriate sequencing of major programs
- Managing risk mitigation across the enterprise
- Identifying and resolving critical project-related issues

PPM provides a centralized and balanced view of various projects, making it possible to select among them and create an optimal investment portfolio. Through a centralized view of all technology projects, a good portfolio will make it easier to ensure that investments are well balanced in terms of size, risk, and projected benefit. Used wisely, it will increase technology's value by exposing projects that are redundant or risky while revealing how to shift funds from low-value investments to high-value, strategic alternatives.

PPM leads to smarter decisions, improving the allocation of resources and reducing project failures. For example, in the early days of the internet, Sun Microsystems decided to move its entire business onto the web, initiating more than 100 internet projects that differed significantly in systems, design guidelines, and protocols. Sun eventually realized that this approach made it impossible to balance project risks and optimize its use of resources. Accordingly, top management adopted a portfolio approach. Sun ended up converting its 100 internet projects into a coordinated, manageable portfolio of about 15 initiatives.

PPM reduces technology costs by eliminating unnecessary projects and management activities that do not add value. Executives at Guardian Insurance estimated that PPM reduced overall applications expenditures by 20 percent, resulting in a decrease in maintenance costs from 30 to 18 percent. The director of enterprise governance at AXA Financial Inc. estimated that PPM saved his company $5–10 million in the first year alone.

PPM improves collaboration between business and technology in several ways. It creates a "single view of the truth" about a firm's operations and generates a common vocabulary and set of metrics. It permits a comprehensive set of decisions to be made in a formal management process before action is taken, proactively identifying and resolving conflicts. It allows strategic direction to flow down to meet suggested courses of action flowing up. PPM is, in fact, continuous: Strategic planning informs portfolio managers, who reassess programs and projects. Information on the status of digital assets, risks, and financial performance likewise influences subsequent strategic planning.

PPM provides information that links business needs with technology activities—enabling a converged viewpoint that is focused on business outcomes, rather than advancing the interests of one group versus another. PPM allows an organization to get beyond the incomplete approach of computing the ROI of individual projects. With a portfolio viewpoint, the payback of a project can be evaluated within the context of many projects contributing to an overall business goal. The merits of individual projects are not seen in isolation, but rather in consideration of their contribution to business capabilities that enable a comprehensive strategy. In forward-thinking companies, business and technology portfolios become inseparable from other portfolios—R&D, new products, and the like—and become just another component of a business initiative.

THE ANATOMY OF A PORTFOLIO

Portfolios, each with different "views," should be created to support different types of activity at various levels within the organization, as depicted in Figure 10.1.

Portfolios of assets and activities provide an enterprise-wide perspective for executives and managers to ensure that the organization is deploying resources to meet its business objectives.

Asset-related portfolios, for example, include technology assets and other (nonfinancial) assets:

- *Technology asset portfolios* include business applications and tools, data, and infrastructure (that is, hardware, operating systems, systems software, etc.).

- *Other (nonfinancial) asset portfolios* include an organization's human resources, the business processes it performs, and the intellectual property it owns.

PORTFOLIO TYPES

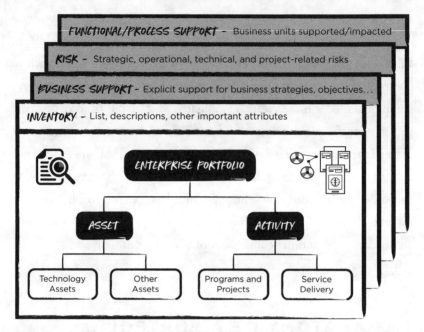

Figure 10.1. Sample portfolio types. Different portfolios should be defined for a variety of business and technology management purposes, ranging from accurately inventorying technology assets to managing strategic risk.

Activity-related portfolios consist of distinct projects, programs, and efforts related to continuous service delivery:

- *Project-level portfolios* include planned undertakings of related activities, including a beginning and conclusion, to reach an objective. Having an enterprise portfolio of projects available to executives and managers enables better monitoring and exception-based management by allowing issues to float to the top. For example, a dashboard providing project-level red/yellow/green indicators across dimensions such as schedule, cost, scope, risk, and governance allows executives to focus on the exceptions instead of spending their time gathering and reviewing reams of data on all projects.

- *Enterprise project portfolios* help with a variety of other activities, such as decision-making, by helping to identify synergies and redundancies in projects or requests; knowledge asset reuse through identification of opportunities to recycle intellectual property assets produced on related projects; and resource and demand management by providing accurate and timely information on project-related demand.

- *Program-level portfolios* include groups of related projects that all need to be completed to reach a certain level of benefits, and which are managed in a coordinated way to obtain a level of benefits and control not available from individual management. For example, a program to improve customer retention via the internet might contain such projects as website redesign, implementation of a new CRM process and tool, and execution of an email marketing campaign. Program managers would ensure that the interdependencies among these projects are well understood, manage risk that cannot be addressed by individual project teams, and deal with other issues such as resource balancing across projects. Having a program view, with linkage to the underlying projects available to executives and managers, enables effective and timely oversight.

- *Service delivery portfolios* include the operational, non-project–related efforts required to support business operations. This is a critical piece of the overall pie when analyzing how well the organization is performing and whether the company is working on the right things based on business objectives. This information is also critical when examining the enterprise resource portfolio and planning for changes to meet demand.

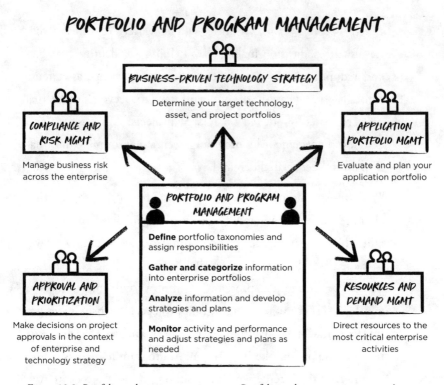

Figure 10.2. Portfolio and program management. Portfolio and program management's impact extends well beyond its core focus.

As illustrated in Figure 10.2, the intelligence and perspectives PPM generates become an integral part of strategy creation, application management, resource and demand management, project approval and prioritization, and compliance and risk management.

Compliance and Risk Management

PPM supports compliance and risk management capability by assisting in the definition of enterprise risk types and related portfolio structures, analyzing organizational vulnerabilities and business objectives, developing generic risk mitigation approaches, and gathering enterprise risks and categorizing them into risk portfolios. These portfolios might label risk as strategic, operational, technical, or project related. PPM also supports compliance and risk management by allowing executives to review an overall enterprise risk map, which provides the ability to analyze and prioritize the risks to be mitigated.

Business-Driven Technology Strategy

With regard to business-driven technology strategy, PPM aids in gathering information on the enterprise business strategy, its objectives, and desired capabilities. It does so by creating portfolios of current enterprise applications, data, and infrastructure assets and architecture, along with portfolios on current and planned enterprise initiatives. PPM also allows the evaluation of technology assets and technology initiatives (existing and planned) against business objectives. It identifies technology enablers to help shape business strategy and guides the development of target architecture vision for applications, data, and infrastructure.

Resource and Demand Management

PPM improves resource and demand management capability through the creation of supply portfolios that identify resources and skills and their availability and allocation. A project demand portfolio should likewise be established for prioritized potential initiatives, planned initiatives, and currently active initiatives. An ongoing operational demand portfolio should be established for problem resolution, minor enhancements (non-project), service requests, and other maintenance and general support. Using these supply and demand portfolios facilitates an effective assessment of the balance of risk and reward, as well as performing resource allocation and balancing. This includes assessing utilization and performance, determining a desired target resource portfolio, and planning resource portfolio adjustments.

Approval and Prioritization

PPM supports approval and prioritization by evaluating the expected business value of different projects, as well as the potential project risks. In supporting this task, program, project, and risk-assessment portfolios can be built that address evaluation criteria such as project complexity, project uncertainty, the stability and quality of technology development groups, and ultimately the expected business capabilities that will be enabled.

The Four Activities of PPM

Many companies are not prepared to adopt a portfolio-level perspective or manage the interdependencies among a large number of initiatives. Often, technology executives think of portfolio management as strictly a project-based exercise, a province of the technology department with little connection to the rest of the business. Effective PPM capability, however, can be achieved only through a balanced and thorough focus on organization structures, processes, information, and automation.[2]

Activity 1–Create structures, define taxonomies, and assign responsibilities

A successful PPM capability requires that the right processes be performed by the right people across the organization at different levels.

Ideally, an Enterprise Program Management Office (EPMO) under the chief information officer (CIO), chief transformation officer, or a chief innovation officer. will assume responsibility for managing portfolios, programs, and projects. Its responsibilities include educating the company and collaborating with key constituents on PPM processes. This group also ensures that the organization has the appropriate tools and information available to perform portfolio analysis. It's also the source of an accurate inventory of initiatives and assets. The EPMO exercises control in defining and overseeing project justification and prioritization; it is the operational owner of project resources and is responsible for the allocation for scarce resources. This includes defining project management approaches and ultimately offering project-level oversight.

Owners, stakeholders, and customers of the EPMO include the Office of the CIO, Office of Architecture and Standards, and line of business executives. The CIO functions as sponsor and reviewer, and in many cases, a chief financial officer of technology also participates as a reviewer. Collectively, the owners and stakeholders must execute PPM in a way that ensures that project risks are being managed, process designs meet objectives, applications and requirements support processes and standards, and target architectures are being followed.

The chief information officer, chief innovation officer, chief digital officer, chief transformational officer, chief technology officer (CTO), and other CXOs are customers of information provided by the EPMO, although much of their work is done in other bodies. A Business Technology Council (a cross-functional group of senior executives), for example, might be where these executives review the organization's portfolios for strategic fit. This group owns the overall strategy, ensuring that the portfolio of technology investments is in sync with the company's strategy and objectives and that major initiatives are receiving the right level of business sponsorship and attention.

A leadership team in the Office of the CIO should exist to review project requests submitted by divisional project approval committees. It can evaluate such requests against enterprise-wide business objectives, strategies, target architectures, and standards while ensuring that the project is appropriately coordinated with similar initiatives. This leadership team should report its project approval decisions to the Business Technology Council.

Divisional project approval committees can use portfolio information for their slice of the business to evaluate, prioritize, and select technology investments, annual operating plans, and out-of-cycle projects. Divisional CTOs and CIOs would participate and provide an enterprise perspective into the group's efforts. This group would also identify a business sponsor and a project steering committee.

At the project level, project steering committees, with members from business and technology, would ensure adequate business and technology project resources, provide project-level oversight, participate in stage-gate reviews, provide authorization to proceed, resolve critical project issues, and escalate issues as needed to the Business Technology Council.

Activity 2—Gather and categorize information into enterprise portfolios

A process of discovery needs to take place—one involving an inventory of company assets and activity. This information-gathering step must be orchestrated effectively because it is no trivial undertaking. Portfolios will support the activities performed by executives and managers in the organization. While creating portfolios, it is critical that these activities be examined in detail so that *customized* portfolios can be created for these users.

A CIO, for example, might have these regular responsibilities (among others): monitoring high-risk projects, collaborating and providing status reports to business leaders (some of whom may be in other countries), managing the overall budget, and collaborating with the organization's technology investment board to allocate investment dollars. To perform these tasks, the CIO would need a portfolio categorized by risk level and by country, one containing all initiatives, and one categorized by investment type (see Figure 10.3). There is no one correct set of portfolios; they should be customized to the strategic needs of the company and the decisions executives must make.

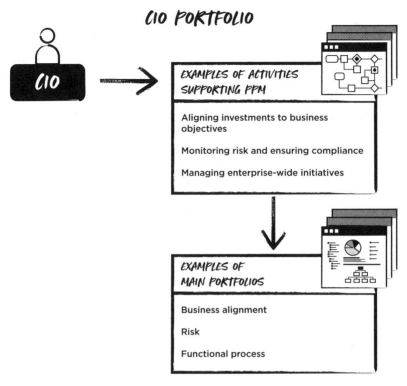

Figure 10.3. Typical CIO supporting portfolios. Portfolios should be created to support various decision-makers, such as the CIO. Business alignment, risk, and process portfolios are among the portfolio types used by a CIO.

Activity 3—Analyze information and develop strategies and plans

The actual analysis of portfolio information will vary depending on the area of activity. For example, if the Business Technology Council is evaluating out-of-cycle project requests, the aggregate investment portfolio might be examined to determine alignment with the company's portfolio investment strategy. If, at the outset of the year, the company planned to allocate spending at 50 percent to infrastructure, 20 percent to transaction processing, 20 percent to decision support, and 10 percent to strategic projects, their approval and prioritization decisions should support this distribution.

Another situation could see the company developing its business-driven technology strategy and, as a result, attempting to allocate resources to support the strategy over the next three years. In this case, the resource supply and demand portfolios would be analyzed to develop an appropriate balance of risk and reward given the desired business and technology targets.

Activity 4—Monitor operations and performance

PPM analytics should support the automatic roll-up of detailed data, which helps to shift the focus of managers from the administrative task of gathering and summarizing data to analysis and exception-based monitoring and decision-making. As in activity 3, the actual monitoring that should be performed will depend on the specific area of activity.

After portfolios are created, taxonomies are defined, and information is categorized to support decision-making, performance metrics should be used to measure the effectiveness of the portfolio. You can use a variety of metrics to track performance. These metrics are typically organized into categories such as financial (economic cost and benefit), business impact (contribution to business performance), risk (likelihood of success or failure), and architectural fit (compatibility with guidelines).

NEED TO KNOW:

- Consider using a portfolio approach to make certain that all technology receives adequate financial support to remain aligned with core business objectives.
- Educate senior executives and start small. Begin to educate senior business and technology executives about the benefits of a portfolio approach. Consider developing a PPM

capability for a small slice of the business to demonstrate the benefits and build consensus for embarking on an enterprise-wide effort.

- Establish management commitment and vision. Most of PPM implementation is not technical but managerial, and the commitment and strategic vision of top executives should be established and sustained. PPM involves many different people needing to do things differently within the organization and must be supported by senior management to achieve success.

- Address new organizational structures early on. Plan the creation of an Enterprise Program Management Office (EPMO), which in most cases owns PPM. The EPMO's responsibilities need to include educating the company on PPM processes and collaborating with key constituents to establish portfolio management approaches. This group will also provide the tools to analyze portfolios and gain access to the inventory of programs, initiatives, and assets. Additionally, create a Business Technology Council, the upper-level strategic decision-making body.

- Design information management processes explicitly. PPM will be an outright failure if the information gathering is not performed adequately from the outset and not kept up to date. Specific processes and responsibilities related to the creation, approval, and updating of information are critical.

CHAPTER 11

TAKE OFF

THE TIME HAS FINALLY arrived for execution.

After what likely amounts to extensive planning, legwork, research, evaluation, and countless other tasks, you're ready to begin the actual implementation of your organization's *Transformation*. Your complete *Transformation* strategy and related plans have been approved. It's an exciting, exhilarating moment, one that, after all the preparation that preceded it, you're confident will prove to be all that you could possibly hope it will be.

But, however heady the moment, don't lose sight of the overriding methodology that got you to this point—a systematic, step-by-step approach, taking on tasks and responsibilities in a thoughtful, sensible chronology. However tempting it may be to push through your reinvention as quickly as possible, don't risk compromising your success with haste.

Thus far, you have had a path forward. Now you need a fine blueprint or an enterprise architecture for execution.

The increased demand on firms to sense and respond quickly to changes in their environments requires a strategic enterprise architecture (SEA) to enable business agility.

Developing an SEA will bring essential order to the islands of information in large organizations. SEA can also serve as the basis for a service-oriented architecture (SOA).

Being agile requires sense-and-respond capabilities that are shaped by designing and managing business processes and technology enablers together.

Processes in most companies are unmanaged, invisible, and unmeasured and are consequently executed haphazardly and inconsistently. This results in delays, errors, low quality, and high overhead costs. The service-oriented business execution model (SOBEM) is a way of organizing the elements, models, and architecture components that help to design processes for agility.

WHY BUSINESS PROCESSES MATTER

Changes in technology and business are dramatically reshaping the process and management capabilities companies require, as well as the means through which they are enabled by technology. Three trends are significant:

- First, business activities are increasingly connected through global business networks, offering new opportunities for horizontal integration and information sharing across organizational boundaries. This trend opens up new opportunities but also makes it difficult to manage effectively from a single center of authority based on one firm's interests.

- Second, technology is becoming ubiquitous—embedded in activities, machinery, products, and services—making it possible to collect data about business processes and outcomes seamlessly. This facilitates the vertical integration of objects and data and creates the technological basis for the real-time enterprise.

- Third, models such as the SOBEM make it possible to conceive an overall business process as a collection of lower-level services and to manage them in response to customer needs.

These trends emphasize the importance of adopting a holistic perspective for horizontal and vertical processes. Only then can senior management follow the interactions between activities end-to-end across organizational boundaries, support efficiency, and explore new opportunities.

Rapidly changing environments require firms to adapt quickly. Some changes relate to incremental modifications in customer preferences, technologies, and markets; these can typically be predicted and prepared for. Others, such as technological breakthroughs (AI, 4IR), terrorist attacks (as they impact security), government interventions (Sarbanes–Oxley), and mergers between firms (as they impact infrastructure integration), require firms to reconfigure processes and technology infrastructures in unpredictable ways. The increased demand on firms to be able to sense and respond quickly requires the creation of an SEA. An SEA is a robust description of a firm's business strategy and the technology that supports it.

HOW FIRMS DEVELOP BUSINESS AGILITY

Success requires innovation in services and products, as well as the continuous improvement of business processes internally and externally. These two mandates mirror one another. Innovation of services and products cannot occur without well-defined and aligned processes, and business processes cannot be improved without attention to changes in customer needs.

An SEA includes the capabilities necessary to design the enterprise from business, process, application, data, and infrastructure perspectives. These are the *business architecture* (business strategies, operating models, and processes) and *technology architecture* (applications, data, and infrastructure) capabilities.[1]

STRATEGIC ENTERPRISE ARCHITECTURE

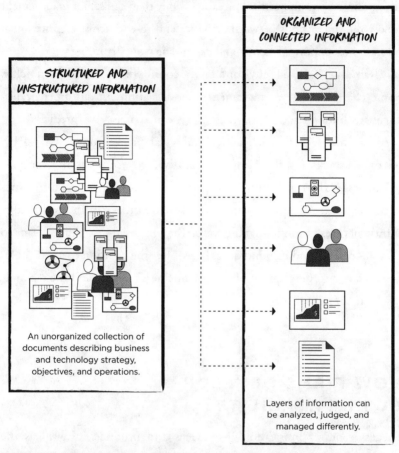

Figure 11.1. Strategic enterprise architecture. SEA transforms structured and unstructured information by organizing and aligning it.

Organizations have used a variety of resources to document bits and pieces of how they operate over time, yet much of this information can be disjointed, incomplete, and of little value. This is often the result of incomplete architecture or absence of commonly accepted standards and terminology, making it difficult to formulate a cohesive picture of the business and technology architectures.

AGILITY INTRODUCES NEW CHALLENGES

Agility is a new paradigm for the production and distribution of services and products. It achieves economies of scope, rather than economies of scale. To be agile, firms must serve ever-smaller niche markets and individual customers without the high cost traditionally associated with customization. Being agile requires sense-and-respond capabilities that are shaped by designing and managing business processes and technology enablers together. Two requirements express the challenges managers face:

- *Sense-and-respond capability*: To respond to changes in their environment, firms must facilitate learning from various processes. This learning must operate at different levels and within different areas of the organization and should be based on recurrent sense-and-respond cycles. Technology can facilitate these learning processes by supporting the collection, distribution, analysis, and interpretation of data associated with business processes, as well as supporting the generation of response alternatives, decisions on appropriate courses of action, and orchestration of selected responses.

- *Improvement and innovation emphasis*: Business agility combines improvement and innovation responses (see Figure 11.2). Opportunistic firms emphasize improvements but often fail to foster innovations. They follow best practices, listen to the customer, and are good at improving current capabilities. Innovative firms, by contrast, are focused on innovating processes through new technologies, services, and strategies. They generate "next" practices but have a limited focus on fine tuning current operations. Fragile firms lack both the ability to identify and explore opportunities and the ability to innovate. When market pressures are high and the environment is turbulent, the ideal is an agile organization that combines improvement and innovation initiatives to constantly reposition itself.

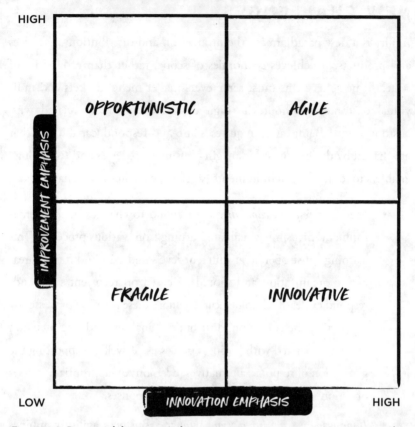

Figure 11.2. Response-ability states. Agile organizations can improve existing practices and innovate new ones.

DISTRIBUTED AND COORDINATED AUTHORITY

Agile firms must adopt radically different forms of governance and translate their mission and objectives into information that can easily be interpreted by constituents. These firms must replace traditional command-and-control approaches with mechanisms that facilitate coordination within and across locales. These mechanisms must provide individuals, groups, and units the autonomy to improvise and act on local knowledge while orchestrating coherent behavior across the firm. Also, processes (who or what does what to whom or what and with what) must be supplemented with personal accountability (who owes what to whom and by when).

Regardless of where one begins the journey toward agility, one quickly encounters the issue of having to align processes of business networks and the information service architecture that supports them.

SOBEM represents frameworks, models, and architecture that reflect the fundamental aspects of a business process perspective. The need for improved business agility can be achieved, in part, through an SOBEM perspective. One can explicitly design agile or less-agile processes through choices regarding process architecture and governance. The SOBEM model can help executives implement *business architecture* and *technical architecture* capabilities by aiding in analyzing design questions such as the following: *Where and what kind of information is being sensed? How quickly and by whom? What's the response to this sensory information? How and with what authority?* SOBEM provides the ability to capture sensory intelligence in real time and develop appropriate responses to events in business processes. Similarly, the flexibility offered in process orchestration empowers firms to greatly improve their ability to change how basic processes behave.

SOBEM offers the opportunity for creating both innovations and improvements, as products and services can be framed as responses that are "rented" by a customer to solve a problem as completely as possible. From this perspective, if the deliverable of a process is the solution, what then is the problem, and is it the appropriate problem from the perspective of the target customer? One can think in terms of improving the solution relative to a better understanding of the problem (that is, an incremental improvement), or identifying new customer problems to which innovative, process-based services can be directed (that is, a disruptive innovation).

STRATEGIC ENTERPRISE ARCHITECTURE (SEA)

A business architecture allows an organization to express its key business strategies and their impact on business functions and processes. Typically, business architecture comprises both current and future state models that define how the organization maintains its competitive advantage. Business architectures are then linked to technology architectures that include applications, data, and infrastructure elements. These elements compose the SEA.

SEA is important in achieving a real-time business network, but it is not sufficient in itself. Also necessary is architecture that represents the various business processes and subprocesses as manageable components used to create an overall business process. SEA sets the context to determine the various services that are required to support the business initiatives. These services form the basis of an SOA.

A service is a business function (for example, a check credit) with an interface that interacts with other services via a loosely coupled, message-based communication model. Services can consist of coarse or polished components, business functions within existing application suites, or actions taken by people. At the highest level, service orchestration is the end goal of process descriptions.

Business process models capture the overall business process logic down to the level of a services orchestration language specification. Ideally, this is done in a way that business rules are separated from the execution syntax to allow the overall business process to be dynamically reconfigured.

Below the level of services, we find preexisting components, objects, and application suites that compose a firm's current application portfolio. These must be encapsulated and given service abstractions that, in turn, allow their orchestration. New process functionality is added directly as services are intentionally designed to work in an SOA.

SEA AND SOA

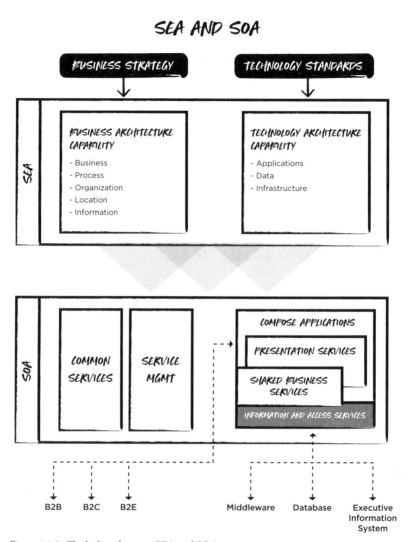

Figure 11.3. The linkage between SEA and SOA.

At the interface between the layers and within the layers themselves, we find a variety of standardized but evolving protocols that aim to increase interoperability across platforms and firms. Standards exist for everything from defining and locating a service description to requesting a web service invocation to managing various aspects of orchestration and additional protocols for security, quality of service, and monitoring.

Beyond service orchestration, however, there is also a mediation component to service interoperability: the task of translating between information models and data models, and the translation of documents and messages into the correct format for interaction with existing applications and infrastructure. And, of course, many other issues need to be addressed, including service quality, security, data consistency, and integrity, to name a few.

FOURTH INDUSTRIAL REVOLUTION (4IR)

Now that you have much of methodology, support, and planned execution in place, let's get some baseline on where technology is today.

As I wrote in my previous book *LIFT*, sweeping change is everywhere, much of it focused on technology. Labeled the "Fourth Industrial Revolution" (4IR), emerging technologies and their interactions with one another are upending how we work, play, educate, and govern ourselves. Artificial intelligence, augmented reality, big data, 3D printing, and the development of various collaborative tools such as *cobots*—robots designed to interact physically with human beings in a collaborative environment—are just a sampling of the power and pervasiveness of technological disruption.

But 4IR is not only about smart, connected machines and systems. Its scope is much wider. For instance, waves of further breakthroughs are occurring at the same time in areas ranging from gene sequencing to nanotechnology and quantum computing.

It is the fusion of these technologies and their interaction across the physical, digital, and biological domains that is transforming how we work, play, live, and communicate.

For something so impactful and widespread in its ramifications, 4IR can seem rather "fuzzy" to many. That's because the optimal term often associated with this explosion ("event" seems an inadequate description) is blurry. Unlike more autonomous forms of disruption and transformation, 4IR is blurring the lines that historically separated physical, biological, and digital arenas. Easy compartmentalization is no longer the rule.

As with its predecessors, 4IR marks a continuation of the disruption that preceded it. Leveraging power generated through water and steam, the first Industrial Revolution introduced mechanized production. The second employed electric power to create mass production. The third used electronics and information technology to automate production.

Now a fourth Industrial Revolution is building on the third—the digital revolution that has been occurring since the middle of the last century. But rather than focusing just on digital growth, 4IR is driven largely by the convergence of digital, biological, and physical innovations. The rise of AI, robotics, the Internet of Things (IoT), autonomous vehicles, 3D printing, nanotechnology, biotechnology, and quantum computing are all elements of this massive union of technology and accessibility.

But the fourth iteration differs from the prior revolutions in a number of other meaningful, impactful ways. Perhaps most distinctive and significant is the exponential speed with which change and disruption are occurring. Given that so much of that change is focused on technological innovation and implementation, which, in turn, fuels and drives change in other areas, the momentum of 4IR essentially nurtures itself, accelerating both the speed of disruption and the scope of its import.

Let us consider some specific forms of technology above and beyond what is discussed in previous chapters that can help you achieve your very specific business objectives. Granted, it can be a lengthy list, but following is a breakdown of issues and areas for possible inclusion:

- *Big data*: Big data is a term that describes the large volume of information, both structured and unstructured, that inundates a business on a day-to-day basis. Although the term suggests that the amount of data is most important, what really matters is how organizations can collect and analyze this information to make better decisions. While the term "big data" is relatively new, the act of gathering and storing large amounts of information for eventual analysis is ages old. The concept gained momentum in the early 2000s when industry analyst Doug Laney articulated the now-mainstream definition of big data as the three *v*'s:

o *Volume*: Organizations collect data from a variety of sources, including business transactions, social media, and information from sensor or machine-to-machine data. In the past, storing it would have been a headache, but today, new technologies have minimized the challenge.

o *Velocity*: Data streams in at an unprecedented speed and must be handled in a timely manner. RFID tags (a tracking system that uses smart barcodes in order to identify items), sensors, and smart metering are driving the need to deal with torrents of data as efficiently and promptly as possible.

o *Variety*: Data comes in all types of formats, from structured numeric data in traditional databases to unstructured text documents, email, video, audio, stock ticker data, and financial transactions.

Big data has three primary sources:

• *Streaming*: This includes material that derives from a variety of connected devices, such as the Internet of Things.

• *Social media*: Social interaction can provide a wellspring of insight and information.

• *Public data*: This is information from federal, state, and local agencies, the European Open Data Portal, and other publicly accessible repositories.

Examples of the use of big data include governmental analysis of information to maintain varied infrastructures, manufacturers finding ways to increase productivity and minimize waste, and health-care providers' use of big data to offer improved patient care.

- *Artificial intelligence (AI)*: AI is a prime example of a pervasive buzzword whose commonly accepted meaning blurs its true value and implications. For many of us, AI means computer systems built to perform tasks normally associated with human intelligence, such as decision-making and speech recognition. This is not entirely correct. A more accurate definition focuses on goal-oriented adaptive behavior geared toward better outcomes—not just reaching a goal but finding the optimal way to do so and learning from any mistakes along the way. Now apply that to the matters of your organization—how can AI be leveraged to make better decisions faster in a replicable fashion that also improves over time?

- *Cloud computing*: A well-known but nonetheless valuable digital tool, this involves the use of remote servers to store, manage, and process data, rather than storing data on-site. Not only can cloud storage adapt to meet changing needs and respond faster to market demands, but off-site storage is also inherently safer than maintaining valuable material in-house.

- *Cybersecurity*: In these days, when major cyber breaches are becoming all-too-common news, it only makes sense to give cybersafety serious consideration as a part of digital transformation. But security isn't the only benefit. For one thing, enhanced safety can offer your colleagues and teammates greater flexibility in using the internet, confident that they're protected from potential threats. Moreover, since hacks and viruses can cripple productivity and innovations, greater cybersecurity helps organizations perform to their fullest capacity.

- *Blockchain*: In a nod to collaboration, blockchain technology is a shared database that exists on many computers at the same time. With "blocks," users can add to the overall chain by sharing new material and information. Since all users on the blockchain must agree on any new additions, transparency and responsibility are paramount. Likewise, the same consensus-based system boosts security, as well as the capacity to trace where certain material came from.

- *The Internet of Things*: The Internet of Things (IoT) is the extension of internet connectivity into physical devices and everyday objects. Embedded with electronics, internet connectivity, and other forms of hardware, these devices can communicate and interact with others over the internet and can be remotely monitored and controlled. Among other pluses, machinery and other tools can effectively "report" when they're in need of service or repair and request appropriate action.

- *Digital marketing*: Taking in all marketing activities that employ electronic devices or the internet, digital marketing allows companies to reach far more consumers than more traditional strategies. In addition to being more cost-effective, digital marketing is also inherently self-analytic, pinpointing what elements are effective and which are less so.

- *3D printing*: The ability to build three-dimensional objects using computer-assisted design allows companies to more quickly manufacture goods that are more cost-effective and have fewer errors. That translates to a significant competitive advantage.

- *Drones*: Here, you may well wonder whether your thinking about digital transformation has jumped the rails. Not so. Not only can drones be used to move products from one location to another, but they're also understandably handy for visual security and capturing images.

- *Robots*: See the discussion on drones. Not only can robots come in more forms than you might be aware of; their uses and advantages are varied, including lowered costs, better work quality and accuracy, and, increasingly, the ability to perform surprisingly complex tasks.

- *Virtual reality*: Basically, this is the creation of a simulated environment. While at first glance, this may seem little more than an extravagant toy, VR improves product prototyping by advancing evaluation and function. It is also cost-effective, as virtual stores can be set up faster and less expensively than their brick-and-mortar counterparts.

- *Augmented reality*: This combines the real with the virtual, involving computer-generated content that is overlaid onto a real-world environment. This tool can be particularly effective in creating a buzz among customers looking for unique experiences. It's great for generating social media chatter as well.

- *Web3*: Also known as Web 3.0, this marks the third generation of the ongoing evolution of web technology. Based on the function of the internet that we all know and use, Web3 will place particular emphasis on decentralized applications and blockchain-based technologies. Web3 will leverage machine learning and AI to create more intelligent applications with broader use and flexibility.

- *Metaverse*: Related to the concept of Web3, metaverse refers to a new and more evolved version of the internet. Metaverse's emphasis is on the increased use and availability of online 3D or virtually integrated environments that provide users access to virtual reality and augmented reality experiences. In a manner of speaking, metaverse takes augmented reality to new and more powerful levels, with possible application in sales, marketing, and other areas where customer experience is critical.

PLANNING EACH INITIATIVE IN DETAIL

You have defined your business case and your architecture and assembled your list of priorities—those projects and initiatives that afford the greatest potential to reinvent your organization in the fashion that needs to be in place. You're clear on just what you mean when you discuss specific components. Additionally, as chapter 10 details, you also have a portfolio-based financial plan in place to make certain that everything receives adequate support. Time to dig a little deeper (yet again!) and develop additional planning with which you can begin to track actual activity.

A comfortable place to start is with projected timeframes. How long do you estimate each initiative may take to be fully in place? Moreover, how does the timeframe of one initiative contrast with the timeframes of other core efforts? Figure 11.4 summarizes this nicely.

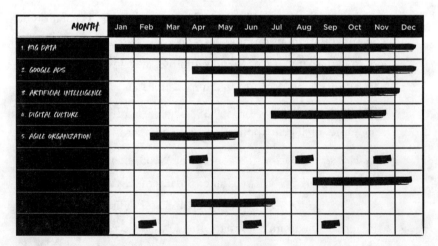

Figure 11.4. Overarching digital transformation plan.

Another, more detailed way to capture timeframes is to delineate individual phases of each initiative. These can involve initial steps, such as designating personnel and hiring additional people, moving on to preliminary implementation of technology, requisite training, and any other steps or milestones that may be involved.

It's never a bad idea to make this as detailed and applicable as possible. Needless to say, what counts as a significant waypoint for one organization may be utterly irrelevant to another. Emphasize those benchmarks and goals that best reflect progress toward the objectives that you've prioritized. The greater the detail and relevancy, the better the chances your organization will keep pace with an optimal timeframe.

For a visual aid, following are some sample road maps for big data and artificial intelligence.

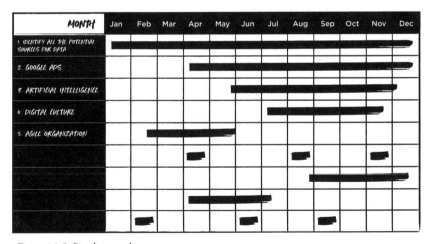

Figure 11.5. Big data roadmap.

SAMPLE DETAILED PLAN FOR "AI"

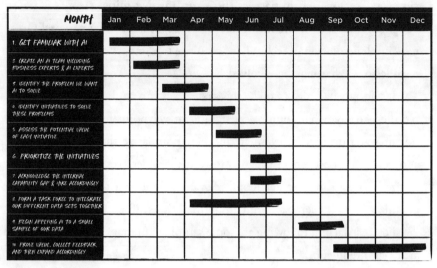

MONTH	Jan	Feb	Mar	Apr	May	Jun	Jul	Aug	Sep	Oct	Nov	Dec
1. GET FAMILIAR WITH AI	███	███	███									
2. CREATE AN AI TEAM INCLUDING BUSINESS EXPERTS & AI EXPERTS		███										
3. IDENTIFY THE PROBLEM WE WANT AI TO SOLVE			███									
4. IDENTIFY INITIATIVES TO SOLVE THESE PROBLEMS				███								
5. ASSESS THE POTENTIAL VALUE OF EACH INITIATIVE					███							
6. PRIORITIZE THE INITIATIVES						███						
7. ACKNOWLEDGE THE INTERNAL CAPABILITY GAP & HIRE ACCORDINGLY						███						
8. FORM A TASK FORCE TO INTEGRATE OUR DIFFERENT DATA SETS TOGETHER				████	████							
9. BEGIN APPLYING AI TO A SMALL SAMPLE OF OUR DATA								███				
10. PROVE VALUE, COLLECT FEEDBACK, AND THEN EXPAND ACCORDINGLY									████	████	████	

Figure 11.6. AI roadmap.

Figure 11.7 lays out one such way to introduce an artificial intelligence initiative. As you can see, the left side of the visual refers to change complexity, starting with relatively little change and moving all the way up to particularly comprehensive change. The horizontal axis addresses who will be affected, ranging from only one particular team to virtually the entire organization (and possibly beyond that).

EXECUTIVE SUMMARY TEMPLATE

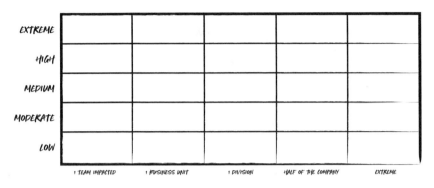

Figure 11.7. Executive summary.

Address the issue of change further by making certain your organization knows the people spearheading the transformative effort, as well as the structure of that particular group. Once again, that promotes greater overall transparency in addition to letting everyone know to whom questions or concerns may be addressed.

NEED TO KNOW:

- Understand the appropriate level of business agility for your organization. Refine and exploit competencies required to operate competitively in strategic positions and strategically reposition your business into new product-market spaces through exploration. Understanding the appropriate level of agility has vast implications for how processes are modeled, configured across business networks, and then enabled by SOA.

- Select modeling approaches for your business processes. New information technologies and architectures (for example, SOA), coupled with SEA and a mandate for agile design, require senior management to reconsider the firm's core processes.

- Create the appropriate level of agility for a business network. Processes must first be established to sense and capture customer requirements and translate them into specifications of outcomes. Second, processes are required to integrate information from the business network and add to the base of public and market information. Third, processes must enable tailoring of interactions, information sharing, and intellectual property protection. Fourth, processes are required for the management of activities associated with production and distribution of products and services, as they must be reallocated and coordinated based on changing conditions. Fifth, governance of relationships must be implemented to enable negotiation and monitoring across activities in business processes and networks. Given the process enablers that are required for the real-time enterprise, it is critical to establish the information services platform required by these processes.

- Develop your SEA functional area. This is absolutely necessary for an agile organization. Technology capabilities must be synchronized with the process requirements of real-time business networks. This synchronization requires senior executives to think primarily in terms of the services they provide and the key business processes and networks that enable, and are enabled by, these services. Senior executives must define the necessary leadership roles, structures, and processes.

CHAPTER 12

STUDY

AS I MENTION SEVERAL TIMES, *Transformation* that incorporates digital technology has no fixed end point. Rather, it is very much a journey, one characterized by constant reinvention, change, and, happily, opportunity.

However tempting it might be to place an exclamation point on a transformative effort, the very nature of the undertaking makes that an unavailable option. But fortunately it does offer the opportunity for study—the last step in one phase of your overall transformative journey.

By study, I mean a comprehensive review of the overall *Transformation* process with digital technology, from the point of initial consideration to the actual execution of all that planning and thinking. This isn't a conventional postmortem—nothing has up and died. In fact, just the opposite. Something has been born, and subsequent study and examination are essential to ensure growth, success, and further evolution.

For one thing, obviously enough, you want to pinpoint what in the journey went right, as well as those times when things didn't exactly go as planned. That unto itself can make subsequent steps in the transformative journey that much easier and more successful—after all, experience is not just the best teacher but the most forthright. It doesn't pull any punches.

Just as important, if not more so, everyone involved wants to know if all the money, resources, and energy that were directed to the *Transformation* were truly worth it. However current and forward thinking many executives may be otherwise, many still cling to a certain skepticism about money and technology. Sure, technology upgrades and improvements certainly seem attractive, but the hefty price tag that many carry can prompt leadership to continuously question if, in fact, all that money poured into technology is truly cost-effective and sufficiently beneficial.

That's why it's important to evaluate and study your own specific situation, rather than measure it against others or industry benchmarks. You need strategies and methodology that allow you to analyze your own experience and outcome with a singular focus.

Still, some outcomes are understandably difficult to quantify. For instance, one particular transformation may emphasize greater digital security. That's certainly worthwhile, but how do you measure the payback? How do you compare money spent with a benefit that doesn't necessarily translate into dollar figures? Likewise for improved decision-making—an indisputable benefit, but something whose advantages can be difficult to plug into a calculator.

But don't focus exclusively on money spent and money earned. It's every bit as valuable to examine your *Transformation* for what it has achieved beyond the realm of dollars and cents. Even though something may not have a monetary value attached to it, that doesn't mean it isn't of significant worth.

This mandates focused, specific methodology geared to evaluating value and commodities that aren't necessarily built to be studied in that manner—and, at the same time, without losing sight of what else has been accomplished outside of financial gain. This chapter offers strategies and ideas with which you can evaluate your own *Transformation*, build confidence that it was, in fact, all worth it and then some, and, just as valuable, sift through your experience to improve the journey forward.

KNOW YOUR OBJECTIVES, THEN BUILD THOSE METRICS THAT FIT

"Are we investing too much or too little in technology?"

All too often, executives answer this question with comparisons to a generic peer group—an approach that can prove increasingly counterproductive the more distinct an organization's business strategies and tactics are from those of others. Only by matching the level and mix of technology investments to its business strategy can an organization be sure it is investing correctly.

Moreover, only part of these investments should be for technology assets such as hardware and software or their application. Equally important is investment in the transformational management capabilities needed to manage the complex relationship between technology and business needs. This means developing the processes, organizational structures, information, and automation necessary for choosing the right technology and implementing it effectively. Without this, investments in hardware and software alone offer little or no value, and efforts to assemble supporting technology are often disconnected from overall business strategy. An organization seeking strategic value from its digital technology must ensure that its technology strategy respects and supports the business strategy.

The objective of technology must be clearly understood before the legitimacy of its value can be established. Metrics for technology benefits must keep up with the changing nature of the business and the technology. Before technology alignment can be effective, the business strategy must be converted into specific activities.

Technology investments cannot occur in isolation. They are among several investments on the way to accomplishing a business strategy. A process approach provides a roadmap for technology impact and value creation, and statistical methods provide the tools to capture, isolate, and measure such impacts.

Top executives can be forgiven for their skepticism about the huge sums they are plowing into technology. Two decades ago, they were alerted to the "productivity paradox," a phenomenon based in part on an observation by the Nobel laureate Robert Solow: "We see computers everywhere, except in productivity statistics."[1] This led to a string of research projects that examined whether and why such was the case. After all, it was counterintuitive that computers would not improve productivity. But if that were the case, should organizations large and small continue to invest in technology?

Subsequent studies attributed the apparent paradox to weaknesses in data and the measurement of technology value. We learned that as technology and business processes change, so must the metrics. This critical insight has yet to be embraced in many executive suites, even today.

This is especially the case for metrics for intangible benefits. For example, it has been reported that since the 1970s, productivity in banks is down; however, the metrics capturing this change were based on the number of transactions per bank teller. We know that technology has played a significant role in enabling online banking and ATMs, so tellers are handling relatively more complicated transactions. Therefore, the metrics must be updated to capture the changing nature of value enabled by technology investments.

HOW TO MAKE SENSE OF TECHNOLOGY'S BUSINESS VALUE

Leaders must clearly understand the objective of technology in their organizations before its business value can be established. Although we use technology as a generic term, it has various and diverse purposes. Attempts to paint all technologies with the same brush can lead to misplaced applications and subsequent disappointment with the payoff.

There are many types of technology investments. Some are meant to ensure compliance, such as with the Sarbanes–Oxley Act of 2002 or the Health Insurance Portability and Accountability Act (HIPAA) for healthcare organizations, the value for which is hardly strategic. Other types of investments are focused on improved decision-making and competitiveness, such as Walmart's purchasing system or Dell's online sales. These are truly strategic and anything but a commodity. Still others prevent security breaches and downtime; although not strategic, these investments have indirect payoffs through risk mitigation.

Therefore, an understanding of the objective and capabilities of technology is the first step in setting goals for expected value.

HOW TO CREATE BUSINESS VALUE METRICS

Once technology objectives are established, metrics can be developed to monitor their value. The suitability of the metrics depends on what is of interest to management—value is in the eye of the beholder. Establishing metrics and agreeing on their validity is to view technology through the beholder's eyes. It is also important to understand that metrics will vary depending on the nature of organizational capability. For example, capabilities such as *approval and prioritization* require metrics that analyze the implications and impact of potential technology investments. Others, such as consolidation and standardization, are used to measure the effectiveness of potential acquisitions or adoption of certain technology standards (for example, databases and application servers). Thus, technology managers should identify key stakeholders and their orientation toward technology. An understanding of the roles and needs of these users will lead to mutually acceptable metrics that accurately measure business value.

For example, Citigroup, the global financial services company, lacked standard processes following the mergers and acquisitions that created its global corporate and investment banking group. A system called Mystic, designed to respond to such issues, provides Citigroup with the capability to track projects, align them with business strategy, and communicate the value to internal customers. Mystic allows these customers to prioritize projects and track their status. Upon completion of a project, both developers and customers rate their satisfaction with each other. This orients technology projects to solving business needs. Consistent with the steps in the preceding examples, an alignment, involvement, analysis, and communication (AIAC) framework can be used so that firms can create a process in which the measurement of technology value is the responsibility of the entire organization.

An information system such as Mystic also enables the transfer of learning among business functions that can help future projects. It provides time and cost estimates so that the business can align strategy with technological capability. It provides actionable steps on how to extract business value from technology and sidestep potential land mines.

Once established, however, metrics must change as the business and technology change. As mentioned previously, productivity metrics in banking must reflect changing customer preferences and technological developments that enable online loan processing and electronic funds transfers, as opposed to old metrics that tracked the number of customers served by a bank teller.

How does one derive appropriate metrics? First, the business mission and profitability model must be well understood. Everyone in the organization must understand how a firm generates revenue and profits, not just those in finance. Metrics established with such an understanding will most likely provide a clear link from technology investment to business value (see Figure 12.1).

Metrics fall into three broad categories: productivity, profitability, and consumer value. Technology's ability to reduce operational costs and improve internal coordination can lead to higher productivity. Improved productivity can lead to higher profitability, but factors such as increased

SELECTING METRICS

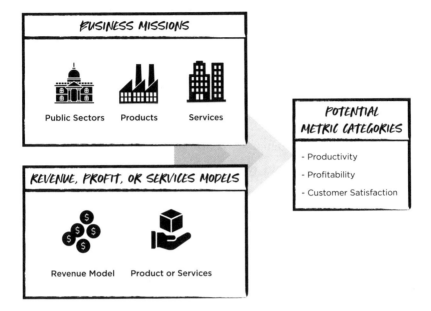

Figure 12.1. Selecting appropriate metrics. An organization's mission and operating models determine the relevant business metrics.

competition and substitute products can offset that. A likely outcome of improved productivity is passing on the gains to consumers through richer features, better service, and improved interaction. Therefore, for each of these categories of metrics, executives must take a holistic approach, understanding all contributors to business value.

VARIOUS ROLES OF TECHNOLOGY

As discussed, technology contributes to business value in several ways. Metrics must be fashioned to capture these contributions. Let's unpack this a bit more. For example, in addition to enabling agility and market alertness, technology creates digital options, such as new ways to build enterprise processes and knowledge systems. Assessing the business value will require metrics to reveal how organizations create agility, sense-and-respond capabilities, and digital options.

Technology investment is also crucial in integrating products with services and products with other products. For example, Schwab, the financial services company, provides trading facilities via phone, the internet, and cell phone. Integration of services that allow customers to access their accounts through a variety of systems requires a significant effort in programming and adaptation to various media.

Otis, through its Remote Elevator Monitoring application, continuously monitors customer elevators and reports problems to technicians, who sometimes respond even before the customer realizes that there is an issue. As another example of knowledge systems and processes that create new digital options, Otis offers a web-based system that enables customers to view information about elevators, such as traffic patterns, security status, maintenance data, and floor accessibility. Clearly, this goes beyond maintenance and repair. The services allow the building owner (for example, a hospital) to understand the origin and destination of visitors. It can then plan on locating other services, such as cafeteria and security, around high traffic areas or vice versa. It can also improve response times by locating physicians and nursing stations closer to elevators. The electronics in the elevators can also be integrated with the hospital's on-call system such that in a medical emergency, as the clinical team's beepers or cell phones ring, the elevators move to where members of the team are expected to be.

Another role stems from corporate privacy transgressions and misconduct, which led to regulations such as HIPAA, the Sarbanes–Oxley Act, and even the Gramm–Leach–Bliley Act, which regulates the sharing of personal information about individuals who obtain financial products or services from financial institutions. This particular legislation also attempts to inform individuals about the privacy policies and practices of such institutions. Each new regulation has contributed to redefining the role of technology in supporting processes and ensuring compliance.

Technology's role in managing the risk from privacy and confidentiality violations is now at the center of its ROI. Section 404 of the Sarbanes–Oxley Act, which requires companies and third-party auditors to document procedures for ensuring the accuracy of their financial statements, is estimated to cost $4.36 million in first-year expenditures for an average public company.[2]

Can we place a value on technology investment in mitigating risk? With investments of such magnitude, metrics for the value of technology must be reinvented.

DEVELOPING THE CAPABILITY TO MONITOR AND USE TECHNOLOGY

As the speed of change has accelerated, so have firms' reaction times. As these reaction times become commonplace, consumer expectations increase. A bank can no longer take three weeks to process an application for a home mortgage loan; neither can an airline wait two weeks to reexamine fares when a competitor lowers its rates. When one credit card company offers variable interest rates, other companies must quickly follow suit in offering flexible payment plans to retain customers.

In each example, an organization must possess capabilities to quickly gather information (sense) and take action (respond). Technology has a unique role in delivering both *sense* and *respond* capabilities (for example, through processing large amounts of data quickly and testing and formulating counter strategies). Interestingly, in many cases, the new products are created by changing accounting and tracking rules. For instance, online home mortgage approvals require replicating loan officers' expertise in a set of knowledge-based rules, credit card variable interest rates require revising the program that calculates interest, and revised fares for an airline require similar change in the origin-destination rate table. Most of these changes are enabled by technology applications (see Figure 12.2).

Organizations continuously gather information to examine changes in both external and internal environments. The changes must then be evaluated for their potential impact on operations. These capabilities require analytical skills to establish the link between business imperatives and

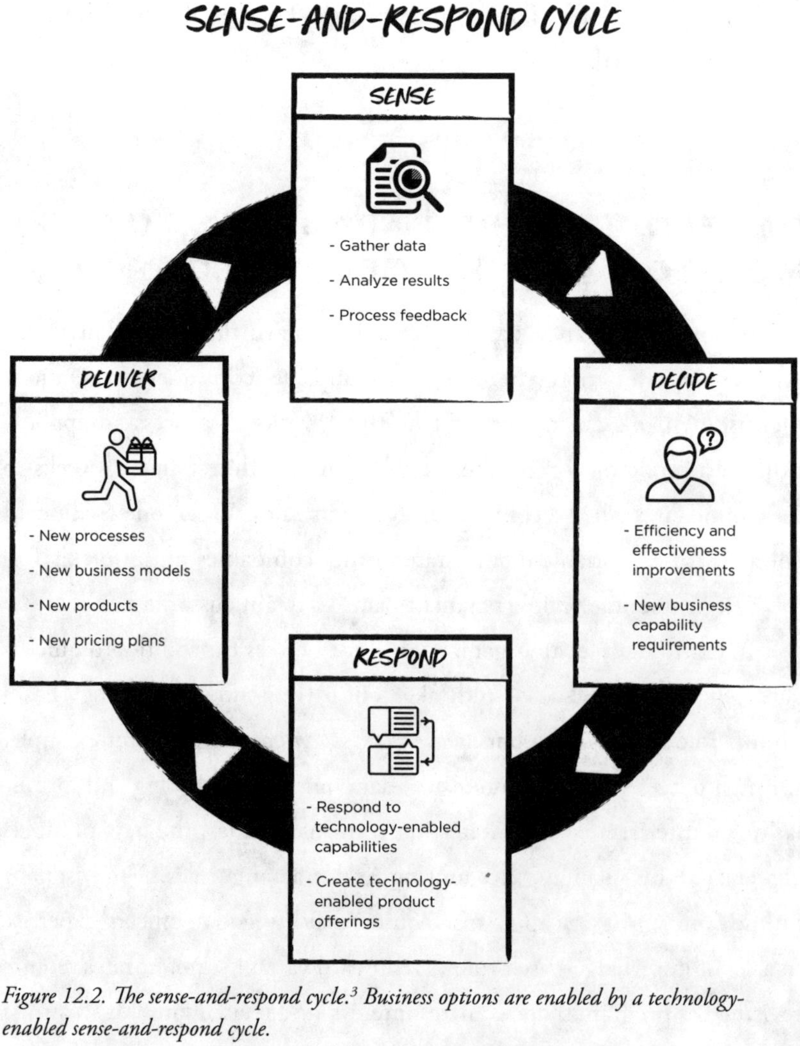

SENSE-AND-RESPOND CYCLE

SENSE

- Gather data

- Analyze results

- Process feedback

DELIVER

- New processes

- New business models

- New products

- New pricing plans

DECIDE

- Efficiency and effectiveness improvements

- New business capability requirements

RESPOND

- Respond to technology-enabled capabilities

- Create technology-enabled product offerings

Figure 12.2. The sense-and-respond cycle.[3] Business options are enabled by a technology-enabled sense-and-respond cycle.

technology initiatives. This requires a deep understanding of the business environment and how strategic changes in the firm's response will address the challenges. Often, the response requires real-time adjustments in operations and strategy, thus placing a greater onus on technology to have a well-oiled system that gathers accurate information and presents efficient business alternatives. The following two examples of technology's role in monitoring changes in external and internal environments demonstrate the importance of creating business capabilities to respond to customer needs.

During the last economic downturn, banks began offering creative home mortgages to keep revenues flowing. The mortgages included products such as low interest in the first five years and adjustable-rate mortgages so that more first-time homebuyers could afford homes. One successful bank continued to operate conservatively and carried the traditional thirty-year home mortgages. As homeowners asked for greater choice and flexibility, the bank's customers—that is, the mortgage companies—warned the bank that they would take their business elsewhere if the bank did not provide flexible new mortgage products within forty-five days. The bank struggled to bring such products to market because it lacked the technical resources to modify mortgage applications and test them before the forty-five-day deadline.

Its competitors, on the other hand, were able to modify their programs and continued to bring new mortgage products to the market by combining their technical prowess with attention to customers' needs. The ability to mesh business expertise with technology capabilities proved to be a winning proposition for these banks. Prior investment in infrastructure set the stage, and a keen sense of customers' changing preferences helped in bringing new products to market. As they sensed change in the marketplace, these banks exploited their expertise to analyze various financial products to meet the new demand. They examined the costs of the technology investment in developing new programs to offer internet-based products and the expected increase in revenue and profitability. Following the decision to proceed, they built real-time metrics modules to analyze the performance of new mortgage products, thus creating a loop for continuous sense-and-respond activities.

The message here is clear. After understanding customers' needs, an organization must turn its attention to exploiting technology to create competencies and the infrastructure for efficiency and cost-effectiveness. On any given day, every technology department has many projects underway, each of which has a relationship to efficiency, improved quality, or better control. In large organizations, however, such projects can become monsters that, at best, delay the delivery of business value and, at worst, actually destroy value.

INCREASING THE VALUE OF TECHNOLOGY INVESTMENT

Organizations can ensure that their technology investments contribute real value in several ways. One way is to identify appropriate complementary investments. It is estimated that for every dollar of technology investment, firms will spend between $5 and $9 in complementary investments. Examples are process innovation and (re)design, governance, reward mechanisms, and training.

In another example, when United Parcel Service (UPS) wanted to achieve total supply chain transparency, it looked to several functions, including information technology, for help. Transparency required integration of various systems: "customer powership," storage and transshipment warehouses, sorting conveyers, and delivery trucks. With this arrangement, the information system serves as the integrating link; however, processes among each system must be streamlined with training and established policies about who, when, and how to input business activity into the information system. UPS deployed an information system that not only provided transparency in the supply chain but, because complementary investments were made, also expanded the scope to extract logistical efficiencies and compliance with stricter post–9/11 federal customs regulations.

Process innovation and (re)design are key complementary investments—lacking them, one runs the risk of merely doing unnecessary things faster. Many organizations now require evidence of process evaluation or redesign as part of requests for new technology funding. The ROI can be significantly enhanced when processes are optimized and technology is targeted to activities or tasks that otherwise take too long, are error-prone, or cost too much.

Three other familiar kinds of complementary investments—training, operational acceptance, and reward mechanisms—are related in that they can be seen to both flow from and be dependent upon one another. A variety of training types, focused on users, managers, and executives, must be available to support a new system. Training is critical to ensure that change occurs smoothly, and training efforts must be customized to directly address the change brought about by technology.

Building on this training, communication about—and sponsorship of—the change must be comprehensive. Efforts made to gain end-user consensus and support of a new system or initiative aid in fostering operational acceptance (actual productive use) of the new system. Establishing reward mechanisms helps to ensure that sponsors and users commit themselves to training, communication, and the swift acceptance of any new system.

Another kind of complementary investment is the creation of systems that continue to reinforce the objectives of senior executives with managers and decision-makers. By ensuring the continued use of a system, its very existence can inform and influence day-to-day decisions and even create peer influence to reinforce the demand for its use.

Organizations can also ensure value by communicating with employees. Although technology is deployed with the objective of improving corporate efficiency and profitability, any new deployment causes disruption and change in work routines. It's natural for people to resist. Without a buy-in and organizational commitment from top to bottom, it is unlikely that the expected payoff will occur.

Sustaining momentum in digital transformation projects is directly related to finding new ways to improve work and business activities. Typically, creative uses of information or insights from a data warehouse originate from a few end users seeking answers to a problem. However, dissemination of such insights can benefit the entire organization. It is important for executives to communicate areas of opportunity where technology can add value. To be effective, these areas of opportunity must be illustrated so that people can relate them to their work activities. This requires that managers understand the business context and frame the insights in the form of customized, actionable steps for the business managers.

Visualize, communicate, orient is the new mantra. Managers should communicate specific examples of how technology made a difference or can make a difference. Here, the chief information officer must partner with other senior executives to raise the "information orientation" of all the people who make up the organization. Companies that have information-oriented cultures emphasize constant improvement in technology practices, information management practices, and—the most often overlooked value—creating information capability, employees' information behaviors, and values (see Figure 12.3).

When an organization has a high information orientation, senior managers perceive that their organization can improve business performance through technology. Organizations in such diverse industries as cement (for example, Holcim) and banking (Citigroup) recognize that raising the information orientation of their senior executives will pay great dividends. These companies focus their resources on information capabilities that make them distinctive. They leverage technology to create new products and services and improve management decision-making.

DIMENSIONS OF INFORMATION ORIENTATION

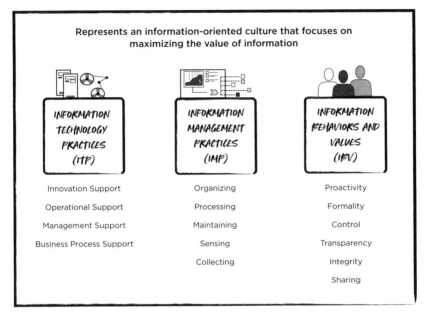

Figure 12.3. Dimensions of information orientation.[4] Organizations display multiple characteristics with regard to their information orientation.

They outsource the rest. In contrast, companies with low information orientation waste their most valuable resources. Such companies never seem to have enough time or people to devote to what is important, because the pressures to do what is necessary always seem to be more urgent.

A good way to determine an organization's information orientation is to benchmark its performance across three critical dimensions identified in Figure 12.3. An organization must focus on all of these dimensions if they want to achieve high business performance.[5] Conducting an information orientation assessment helps establish an enterprise-wide common language or mindset that is crucial to setting the right path for future value improvement.

METHODS, MECHANISMS, AND TACTICS TO MEASURE TECHNOLOGY'S CONTRIBUTION

What are the steps in the technology investment process that provide an opportunity to measure its impact? Several methods and mechanisms are discussed next from a high-level perspective.

A process approach to technology investment can better explain how it creates value for the firm. The process approach involves assessing if (a) proper technology assets were created, (b) the assets led to technology impacts, and (c) the technology impacts led to firm-level impacts. Technology assets and corresponding technology must be aligned with the firm's market position and the competitive environment to see a measurable impact of organizational performance.

The process approach has several implications for measuring technology's contribution to business value. First is that technology investment must be viewed in a business context. Second, this investment must be aligned with business processes that make a difference with business activities. Third, technology must support business activities that take advantage of a competitive position or create a niche position to which the competition must react.

Whereas the process approach provides a roadmap for technology impact and value creation, statistical methods provide the tools with which to measure such impacts. Some statistical methods can also provide analytical support for future investment based on historical data or managerial assumption (see Figure 12.4).

Cost-benefit analysis measures the difference between the investment and returns from that investment. The challenge is to identify and agree on the intangible costs and intangible benefits, which are often a source of discord among stakeholders. For instance, an analysis of the payoff from investment in customer relationship management may reveal higher sales from better tracking of customer leads but overlook the costs of data

STATISTICAL MEASUREMENT METHODS

METHOD	CHARACTERISTICS	USE WHEN	SUPPORTING CAPABILITY
Cost-Benefit Analysis	Seeks to find the surplus of benefits after accounting for cost; does not consider the strategic value of the Investment	Investments have mostly tangible costs and tangible benefits	Approval and Prioritization
Total Cost of Ownership (TCO)	Accounts for all costs—present and future, direct and indirect; TCO can be used as an input into cost-benefit analysis	Investments have longer life span and recurring support expenses (e.g., software licenses, process skills)	Technology Architecture
Net Present Value (NPV)	Measures the contribution of a project after discounting the borrowing costs	Comparing the financial contribution of two or more investments	Portfolio and Program Management
Real Options	Measures benefits or opportunities for benefits beyond the direct benefits. Costs of the options are known but the benefits are contingent upon future conditions	Investment can be staggered; opportunities have uncertain outcomes; investments are for emerging technologies	Consolidation and Standardization

Figure 12.4. Statistical measurement methods.[6] A number of statistical methods support investment analysis.

acquisition or analysis and system maintenance. In another instance, higher sales may be accounted for in the performance of the sales function instead of being attributed to technology, thus leading to incomplete analysis. For this reason, firms are also considering total cost of ownership (TCO) as an approach to quantifying the value of technology. TCO considers all costs over the life of the system when compared to the total benefits. TCO can be time consuming but valuable in that it can help craft certain assumptions about the future.

Net present value (NPV) is a commonly used approach to measure the future value of a current investment by discounting it at a given rate. The rationale for using NPV is that every dollar invested today will be worth less in the future. The reason is that it costs to borrow capital, called the cost of capital, which is incurred through interest and other expenses. In other words, future benefits of today's investment must be discounted by at least the cost of capital, also called weighted average cost of capital (WACC). WACC is commonly at 12–15 percent, implying that the technology investment must yield more than the WACC to return value to the firm. NPV is also an effective tool to compare the relative returns of two or more projects and is often used by managers to prioritize opportunities for investment.

Measuring the business value of future technology investment, particularly in emerging technologies, can be difficult and risky. Because little historical information is available and the payoff depends upon the accuracy of the predictions, the risks as well as opportunities must be accounted for. Given that the potential benefits of technology are harder to define than costs, *real options* methodology proposes that technology investment can be made in stages—that way, the preliminary investment provides a stake as well as a chance to reverse the investment decision.

Drawn from options theory, the real options approach suggests that an initial investment creates future opportunities for the firm. Given favorable market conditions, the firm can exercise the option to make a secondary investment and take advantage of the business opportunity. However, market conditions may remain unfavorable, and the option may not be exercisable. Because the value of the investment in the option is known, firms can choose or decline to bear the risk. Real options methodology is a particularly useful tool when technology is being considered in emerging areas such as electronic commerce and other innovative areas of business.

GETTING THE PAYOFF

For many organizations, the link between technology investment and business performance remains elusive. However, companies that embrace comprehensive information know how to break out of the cycle of spending more on technology and receiving less in return. These companies use technology and management capabilities to leverage information across their business processes and with customers and suppliers to gain knowledge for developing new products, spotting emergent customer needs, forming strategy, and analyzing risk. Such organizations understand that the payoff demands moving the conversation beyond "smokescreen" technical infrastructure issues to the more difficult job of delivering the right information to the right person at the right time.

However, even delivering the right information does not guarantee effective use. To ensure that good information delivery results in a good business outcome, companies must push to instill in their employees precisely those behaviors and values that affect how the company best uses information for customer, supplier, and partner relationships. With this, an information-oriented culture flourishes, and money spent on technology pays off to the fullest extent possible.

NEED TO KNOW:

- Establish the business purpose of each investment in technology: Is it to enable growth, maintain the infrastructure, or manage risk?
- Determine whether the metrics you use have changed along with changes in business processes and technology.
- Agree on new metrics that show how your organization creates agility, sense-and-respond capabilities, and digital options. This agreement will ultimately lead to metrics that accurately measure business value.
- Understand the business environment and how the firm adjusts its strategy to changes in the environment. This often

continued

requires real-time adjustments in operations, placing greater onus on technology executives to have an efficient system to gather information and present business alternatives.

- Leverage approval, prioritization, consolidation, and standardization to manage and define the information requirements to support a highly information-oriented culture.
- Translate business strategy into tactical plans for which information and communication technologies can be deployed. It is increasingly the role of technology executives to make this connection. Executives must take the lead in communicating areas where technology can add value. Employees must be made aware of how these opportunities relate to their jobs.
- Identify complementary investments necessary to get full value out of technology investments.
- Instill in employees the behavior and values that will lead to information for customers, suppliers, and partner relationships.

SECTION 4

SECTION 4

FINAL THOUGHTS

ORGANIZATIONAL *TRANSFORMATION* WITH A significant digital presence is like navigating a major city's subway system. You get on one train, only to get off at the next stop and board another. And so it continues.

But, unlike a hapless visitor clinging to the hope that the next leg will be the final one, you understand that your trip is never really going to end. Organizational *Transformation* is a journey that never stops.

It's up to you to keep steering in the correct direction. Accordingly, staying on the right course with your organizational *Transformation* mandates your continued evolution as a leader as well.

A successful *Transformation* is certainly a testimony to your leadership skills. Not everyone can help devise, implement, and motivate to the level required by sweeping change—the steep failure rate attests to that. And, as an accomplished leader, you're well aware that meaningful change can't possibly take place without equal conviction and energy from everyone on your team. Acknowledged inclusion is everything.

But the challenge is by no means over. As you and your organization move forward, so too must you continue to hone, sharpen, and, if need be, change elements of your leadership. Your organization isn't what it was yesterday—and neither should you stay the same.

One core focus of organizational *Transformation* is greater synergy between silos—those often highly isolated pockets of your company that benefit from more coordination with other areas. As an evolving leader, apply that same sort of thinking to the relationship between technology and business strategy and decision-making.

In one respect, that means building a culture where leadership genuinely listens to and connects with ideas and thoughts from technologists. By the same token, culture also needs to encourage the technology-minded to lose the jargon and work to better convey the value of considering technology in every significant strategic decision. In effect, both sides of the equation need to move closer together in a mutual commitment to supporting one another.

To further expand that pursuit of synergy, consider retooling the nature of leadership positions—in effect, making the tech person responsible for certain business decisions and shifting non-tech leadership toward greater exposure to technology matters. Not only does that build greater diversity of skills and experience, but it also boosts a sense of overall empathy and connection. Business and technology are that much more intertwined and converged. Further, they become a part of a pervasive mindset, one where the two are never far apart.

Leverage the power of greater synergy by applying it to the inevitable issue of money. As I've discussed, organizations of all types have shredded hundreds of millions of dollars on poorly planned and executed swipes at *Transformation*. Although the reasons for those pervasive missteps can vary, one undeniable mistake has to do with finances—an organization's failure to view investment technology as an ongoing factor in the overall direction of the organization.

A leader moving forward in sync with the organization's growth makes certain not only that technology investment is a point of ongoing review and revision but also that it is and remains in line with the company's vision, culture, and other core philosophies. Once more, a potentially destructive silo is dismantled.

It's critical to recognize that as an organization changes and evolves, so must its governance. For one thing, it needs to emphasize greater inclusion and comprehensive participation, including permanent and ad hoc groups and committees—all of which will likely have greater involvement and import than before.

Additionally, there's the recognition of technology governance. As a leader, you'll need to know where technology decisions are being made and who's making them, and, perhaps most important, you'll need to ensure that technology decisions and investments reflect your overall enterprise strategy.

Admittedly, you have a full plate in front of you. But it need not be as intimidating as it might at first seem. Start by prioritizing—focus on the greatest problems, issues, or points of concern and address them first. The sooner you can start showing positive results, the greater the buy-in and support from everyone within the organization.

Moreover, don't assume that your leadership style must be a complete departure from the leader you once were. Like the organization itself, not everything has to be discarded in favor of something different. For example, if you found a particular communications style or system to be effective in the past, there's no need to reinvent it. Rather, improve and hone it further.

Let me conclude by highlighting what my late friend Tom Trainer taught me a very long time ago about future leaders embarking on the journey of *Transformation*. Those lessons are perhaps more valuable now than ever before. He was convinced that leaders of the future must embrace the following:

- *Follow the money.* They must focus on the business and understand how it creates value. Leaders must understand the business strategy: Regarding each product market, is the firm in an exploratory or exploitative posture? This assumes that the organization *has* a strategy that is well articulated and supported by appropriate structures, processes, and information.

- *Know that managing technology is as important as the technology itself.* The next generation of leaders will understand—or should if they want to succeed—that they must invest in managing technology as well as in the technology itself. If there is any remaining doubt today, there will not be in the future; technology, per se, is an equalizer. Only in the management of it can firms eke out an advantage.

- *Understand what technology does.* Unless they appreciate that technology often plays a critical role in establishing or maintaining a strategic position, future leaders may well spend inappropriately. But that appreciation must evolve to an understanding of how the various types of technology—those that enable transactions, decisions, or relationships, for example—contribute to an organization's strategic actions. More often than not, in the first half century of technology, it was thought about only tactically.

- *See through walls.* Tomorrow's leaders will be far more comfortable with deriving value through partnerships and other types of engagements. They must understand the role technology plays in enabling these partnerships and learn to manage the technology that stretches across internal organizational boundaries.

- *Manage business and technology as one.* The moments of dissension and the finger-pointing at failures will disappear as executives come to see that technology failure is often due to weak or nonexistent business strategy or failure to create a business-driven technology strategy. Alignment will increasingly be seen as only the first step; it will occur to all that the design and management of business cannot be done apart from the design and management of technology.

- *Scrap the org chart.* We are already seeing the blending of corporate roles. It will be commonplace in the future. Leaders will have to be comfortable in both the business and technology realms. This re-identity is already underway.

- *Get underneath the hood.* Leaders of the next generation must be able to discern business processes below the overarching posture of an organization that advance strategy. Moreover, they must see technology as part and parcel of these processes; the two are inseparable. This is going to require untying the functional straitjackets in which many organizations have existed.

- *Get comfortable with speed.* Is it too much of a cliché to say that everything will move faster and faster, that interconnectivity makes the whole world our playing field, and that we must give up command and control so that our people on the edges of the organization can react to events in real time? And that this is an entirely new way of thinking about management and leadership? And that even if we pay lip service to it today, it will be very hard to accomplish?

Above all, what really matters moving forward is your understanding and recognition of the scope of change, in which you are a valuable player. Armed with that powerful mindset, you've positioned yourself to be just as aware of how different your organization will look in the future—and how you can adapt to help that journey continue toward growth and further success.

ACKNOWLEDGMENTS

WHEN WRITING A BOOK that is the result of a thirty-year personal and professional journey—one that is made possible by years and years of work with colleagues, customers, partners, academics, and industry experts from around the globe—it is difficult to convey the gratitude I have for all those who have played such an integral role along the way in just a few paragraphs.

First and foremost, I am forever indebted to my late friends and mentors Tom Trainer and Hideo Ito for supporting my thoughts, ideas, and ventures that have helped to create the very foundation of this book.

Next, I thank the customers, partners, team members, and academics who have been applying my methods, processes, frameworks, and platforms. They have driven me to continuously improve upon the pragmatic approaches, solutions, and products we have created to solve the complex problems that industry faces in the campaign for sustainable success. They have empowered me to learn, serve, and grow. I am honored.

I am utterly thankful to my content team, particularly Jeff Wuorio and Shelley Moench-Kelly, for their tireless efforts in researching and editing content with brilliant craftsmanship. Without them, there would be no *REINVENT*.

Thanks to the entire design, editorial, production, and project management team members at Greenleaf Book Group and Fast Company Press, along with my own internal multitalented team members that have made *REINVENT* a reality. Their collective expertise is nothing less than world-class.

Two people, Lori Ames and Paul Berg, have been on my side with the best advice at every step of my journey for decades. I couldn't have written *REINVENT* without their constant support.

I am grateful to my family (near and far) for their unlimited love and support, and there are not enough words for my friends, who are there for me every day.

No one survives in a vacuum. My gratitude extends to those who make our lives easier and help us reinvent when we need it most.

Authors write for readers. Most of all, thank you for reading *REINVENT*.

—**Faisal Hoque**, October 4, 2022

ABOUT THE AUTHOR

 **FAISAL HOQUE IS AN** accomplished entrepreneur; noted thought leader; technology innovator; advisor to CEOs, boards of directors, and the United States federal government; and author with more than twenty-five years of cross-industry success. He is the founder of SHADOKA, NextChapter, and other companies. They focus on enabling sustainable and transformational changes. As a founder and CEO, he is a three-time winner of Deloitte Technology Fast 50 and Deloitte Technology Fast 500™ awards.

Throughout his career, he has developed over twenty commercial business and technology platforms and worked with public- and private-sector giants such as the U.S. Department of Defense (DoD), GE, MasterCard, American Express, Northrop Grumman, CACI, PepsiCo, IBM, Home Depot, Netscape, Infosys, French Social Security Services, Gartner, Cambridge Technology Partners, JPMorgan Chase, CSC, and others. What sets Faisal apart is the unique position and perspective he has always maintained, which is grounded in hardcore technology with deep roots in leading-edge management science.

As a thought leader, he has authored and co-authored ten award-winning books on humanity, business, and technology, including the #1 *Wall Street Journal* and *USA Today* best seller *LIFT: Fostering the Leader in*

You Amid Revolutionary Global Change (Fast Company Press) and the #2 *Wall Street Journal* and *USA Today* best seller *Everything Connects: Cultivating Mindfulness, Creativity, and Innovation for Long-Term Value* (Fast Company Press). His work has appeared in *Fast Company, Business Insider, Wall Street Journal, BusinessWeek*, Fox, CBS, *Financial Times, Mergers & Acquisitions, Forbes, Inc., I by IMD, Leadership Excellence*, and *Huffington Post*, among other publications.

American Management Association named him one of the Leaders to Watch. The editors of Ziff-Davis Enterprise named him one of the Top 100 Most Influential People in Technology, alongside leading entrepreneurs such as Steve Jobs, Bill Gates, Michael Dell, Larry Page, and others. Trust Across America-Trust Around the World named him one of the Top 100 Thought Leaders, alongside global leaders such as Bill George, Doug Conant, Howard Schultz, and others.

His book *The Power of Convergence* (American Management Association) was released in April 2011 and almost immediately was named one of the Best Business Books of 2011 by 800-CEO-READ and *CIO Insight*. Two of his previous books, *Sustained Innovation* and *Winning the 3-Legged Race* (Prentice Hall), were also included in the Top 5 Transformation Books of the last few years, while *Sustained Innovation* also ranked in *CIO Insight* magazine's 10 Best Business Books of 2007. His highly acclaimed book *The Alignment Effect* (Financial Times Press) was published in 2002, and *e-Enterprise* (Cambridge University Press) in 2000.

His broad areas of expertise include innovation, leadership, management, sustainable growth, transformation, strategy, governance, mergers and acquisitions, frameworks, and digital platforms. He holds a strong belief that it is through knowledge sharing that we may provide the greatest clarity on how to improve our collective future. As a globetrotter, he is passionate about nature, people, culture, music, and design, and he loves to cook.

For more info, visit faisalhoque.com or LinkedIn or follow him on Twitter (@faisal_hoque).

Mikołaj Jan Piskorski, also known as Misiek Piskorski, is Professor of Digital Strategy, Analytics and Innovation and Dean of IMD Asia and Oceania. He is an expert on digital strategy, platform strategy, and the process of digital business transformation. He works with companies in various industries across the globe to support them through digital transformation.

Piskorski aims to demystify digital transformation by taking this complex and complicated topic and distilling it down to its core principles, and to the five or six key decisions that companies need to take. The multilayered framework that he developed to help companies devise a digital transformation strategy consists of a series of easy to understand steps. This exercise is made more accessible by the use of cases to show how other companies have tackled the process. Companies come out at the end with a detailed strategy they can implement in full or in part.

One element of digital transformation is the use of social platforms, which Piskorski documented in his book *A Social Strategy: How We Profit from Social Media*, winner of the Axiom Business Book Awards gold medal in 2015. Backed by original research, case studies, and proprietary data from social media sites, the book provides insights on how companies can leverage social platforms to create a sustainable competitive advantage.

Piskorski uses his framework for digital transformation to help companies from a broad range of industries including financial services, automotive, manufacturing, and health care as they seek to tap into the opportunities offered by digitalization. He carries out a lot of work with senior teams, but specializes in transformations that span the entire organization. This approach typically embraces strategic advisory services to the CEO, strategic transformation projects, and business development with the top management team, executive education with middle managers, and online education with the rest of the organization.

At IMD, he leads custom programs for Johnson & Johnson, Telecom Malaysia, the Asian Development Bank, Bayer, SHV, and DNB. In addition, he is the Director of the Digital Strategy (DS) open program and Co-Director of the Leading Digital Business Transformation (LDBT) program. As Dean of Southeast Asia and Oceania, he also runs IMD's activities in the region.

Piskorski's research has been published in *Administrative Science Quarterly,* the *American Journal of Sociology, Harvard Business Review, Management Science, MIT Sloan Management Review,* and *Social Forces.* He is also an associate editor at the *Journal of Organizational Design,* and has served on the editorial boards of several academic journals including the *American Journal of Sociology, Administrative Science Quarterly, Management Science,* and *Organization Science.*

Before joining IMD in 2014 he was Associate Professor of Business Administration at Harvard Business School and started his academic career as a faculty member at the Graduate School of Business at Stanford University.

ABOUT IMD

IMD IS AN INDEPENDENT academic institution with campuses in Lausanne, Switzerland, and Singapore. For more than 75 years, IMD has been a pioneering force in developing leaders who transform organizations and contribute to society.

IMD has been ranked in the top three of the FT's Executive Education Rankings (combined ranking for open & custom programs) since 2012. It has also been in the top five for more than 15 consecutive years.

This consistency at the forefront of its industry is grounded in IMD's unique approach to creating "Real Learning. Real Impact." Led by an expert and diverse faculty, IMD strives to be the trusted learning partner of choice for ambitious individuals and organizations worldwide. Challenging what is and inspiring what could be.

RESEARCH AND EDITORIAL CONTRIBUTORS

Jeff Wuorio

Jeff Wuorio has written more than thirty books covering entrepreneurship, leadership, progressive workplaces, and other similar subjects. His work has also appeared in *Time, BusinessWeek, Money Magazine, Fortune, USA Today*, and many other publications and websites. He lives and works in Maine.

Shelley Moench-Kelly

Shelley Moench-Kelly is a New England–based writer with more than 3,500 published articles and blogs for freelance clients that include Google, L'Oréal Paris, Paramount Studios, Warner Bros., Marvel Comics, TheWeek.com, Prevention.com, LendingUSA.com, Mamapedia.com, and Radisson Blu Hotels. She is a longtime member of the Association of Ghostwriters, the Freelancers Union, and the Authors Guild. Her latest book, *Here's Your Pill, Kitten!*, is available on Amazon.

MORE FROM THE AUTHOR

EMPATHY. KNOWLEDGE. EXECUTION. TRANSFORMATIONAL LEADERS LEVERAGE POSITIVE CHANGE.

In a world of explosive change and transformation, leaders at all levels—from heads of state and global corporations to entrepreneurs and gig economists—will offer the best opportunity for leveraging change and transforming our lives for the better.

This #1 *Wall Street Journal* and *USA Today* best seller invites readers to explore the intersection of transformational leadership, systemic thinking, and experiential learning—all required to survive and thrive the tsunami of changes and disruptions caused by the Fourth Industrial Revolution, the COVID-19 pandemic, climate change, and misinformation trends.

GROUND-BREAKING DIGITAL CLASSES
LIFT OTHERS BY LIFTING YOURSELF

Change and disruption have swelled into a tsunami, carrying enormous consequences and impacts. The question is, Will you be pulled under by these crashing waves of change, or will you choose to adapt and **learn to navigate the stormy seas so the waves lift you up, as well as others along with you**?

Find more information at https://nextchapter.org/lift/.

MINDFULNESS. CREATIVITY. INNOVATION.
A HOLISTIC APPROACH TO CREATING
LONG-TERM VALUE.

In this #2 *Wall Street Journal* and *USA Today* best seller, Faisal Hoque provides a framework that shows readers how to:

- Holistically connect the "when" and "what" with who they are

- Inspire and lead inside and outside of their organization

- Generate ideas, grounded decisions, and long-term value

Part philosophy, part business, and part history, this thought-provoking book explores the intersection of mindfulness, creativity, and innovation. You'll learn from the wisdom of 2,500-year-old Eastern philosophies and the interconnected insights of Leonardo da Vinci. Couple that with Fortune 100 corporate cross-pollination for creativity and start-up thinking for how to adapt with ease, and you have *Everything Connects*. This isn't just a quick fix for your next financial quarter; this is how you succeed in the long run.

GROUND-BREAKING DIGITAL CLASSES MINDFULNESS AND CREATIVITY CREATE A LONG-TERM CULTURE OF INNOVATION

Based on the *Wall Street Journal* and *USA Today* best-selling book *Everything Connects*, Faisal Hoque presents a framework for understanding how the *power of mindfulness and creativity create a long-term culture of innovation* to adapt to our rapidly changing world. You will learn how slowing down deepens your focus and how that practice of mindfulness expands your creative power. Then, with a curious and open mind, you will easily collaborate across the organization and build whole ecosystems of innovation. **These ideas aren't just a quick fix for your next financial quarter; this is how you succeed in the long run.**

Find more information at https://nextchapter.org/everythingconnects/.

NOTES

Preface

1. Finbarr Toesland, "How Five Brands Learned from Digital Transformation Failure," BBC, September 26, 2018, https://www.raconteur.net/digital /digital-transformation-failure/.

2. Couchbase, "Digital Transformation—Lessons Learned and Strategic Setbacks," 2022, https://resources.couchbase.com/c/digital-transformation -report?x=KUOHOP.

Chapter 1—Your Customer Isn't What He or She Used to Be

1. April Berthene, "Coronavirus Pandemic Adds $219 Billion to US Ecommerce Sales in 2021–2022," Digital Commerce 360, March 15, 2022, https://www .digitalcommerce360.com/article/coronavirus-impact-online-retail.

2. Berthene, "Coronavirus Pandemic Adds $219 Billion."

3. Michael Klein, "Online Grocery Traffic Surged up to 300% during COVID-19," *Adobe Experience Cloud Blog* (blog), August 26, 2020, https://business .adobe.com/blog/the-latest/online-grocery-traffic-surged-during-covid19.

4. Russell Redman, "Increased Use of Online Grocery Shopping 'Here to Stay,'" *Supermarket News*, August 25, 2021, https://www.supermarketnews.com /online-retail/increased-use-online-grocery-shopping-here-stay.

5. Redman, "Increased Use of Online Grocery Shopping."

6. Adam Rogers, "17 Trending Products and Things to Sell Online (2022)," *Shopify* (blog), September 12, 2022, https://www.shopify.com/blog/trending -products.

7. Tamara Charm, Becca Coggins, Kelsey Robinson, and Jamie Wilkie, "The Great Consumer Shift: Ten Charts That Show How US Shopping Behavior Is Changing," McKinsey and Co., August 4, 2020, https://www.mckinsey.com/business-functions/marketing-and-sales/our-insights/the-great-consumer-shift-ten-charts-that-show-how-us-shopping-behavior-is-changing.

8. Charm et al., "The Great Consumer Shift."

9. Giorgi Lobzhanidze, "Mastering Customer Loyalty in the Digital Era," *QMinder* (blog), https://www.qminder.com/blog/customer-service/digital-customer-loyalty/.

10. Lindy Nham, "How Do Loyalty Programs Increase Sales?" *3 Tier Logic* (blog), February 25, 2021, https://www.3tl.com/blog/15-customer-loyalty-statistics.

11. Kasey Lobaugh, Jeff Simpson, and Bobby Stephens, "The Changing Consumer: Demographic Forces at Play," Deloitte, October 22, 2019, https://deloitte.wsj.com/articles/the-changing-consumer-demographic-forces-at-play-01571792582.

12. "Online Shopping Statistics and Trends in the USA," Finical, 2022, https://finicalholdings.com/online-shopping-statistics-and-trends-in-the-usa/.

13. Nham, "How Do Loyalty Programs Increase Sales?"

14. Natasha Dailey, "Baby Boomers Flocked to Online Shopping like Never Before during the Pandemic, New Data Shows," *Insider*, January 22, 2021, https://www.businessinsider.com/baby-boomers-e-commerce-fastest-growing-demographic-online-shoppers-2021-1.

15. Lobaugh, Simpson, and Stephens, "The Changing Consumer."

16. Lobaugh, Simpson, and Stephens, "The Changing Consumer."

17. National Retail Federation, *Consumer View Fall 2017*, 2017, https://cdn.nrf.com/sites/default/files/2018-10/RS-005_ConsumerView_0908_Web.pdf.

18. National Retail Federation, *Consumer View Fall 2017*.

Chapter 2—Your Workforce Is Calling for *Transformation*

1. Bureau of Labor Statistics, February 2022.

2. Lucas Mearian, "The Great Resignation: Why Workers Quit (and How Companies Can Respond)," *Computerworld*, December 21, 2021, https://www.computerworld.com/article/3645496/the-great-resignation-why-workers-quit-and-how-companies-can-respond.html.

3. Fell Oliveros, "68% of U.S. Employees Prefer Remote Work Over In-Person Work," ValuePenguin, September 10, 2021, https://www.valuepenguin.com /news/employees-prefer-remote-work.

4. The Execu|Search Group, "The Great Resignation Presents a Powerful Opportunity to Reimagine Employee Experience in 2022, According to New Hiring Report by The Execu|Search Group," PR Newswire, January 11, 2022, https://www.prnewswire.com/news-releases/the great-resignation-presents-a -powerful-opportunity-to-reimagine-employee-experience-in-2022-according -to-new-hiring-report-by-the-execusearch-group-301457630.html.

5. Teevan, J., Baym, N., Butler, J., Hecht, B., Jaffe, S., Nowak, K., Sellen, A., and Yang, L. (Eds.), "Microsoft New Future of Work Report 2022," Microsoft Research Tech Report MSR-TR-2022-3, 2022, https://aka.ms/nfw2022.

6. Morgan Smith, "50% of Companies Want Workers Back in Office 5 Days a Week—Why Experts Say This Strategy Could Fail," *CNBC*, March 18, 2022, https://www.cnbc.com/2022/03/18/50percent-of-companies-want-workers -back-in-office-5-days-a-week.html.

7. Jackie Wiles, "No, Hybrid Workforce Models Won't Dilute Your Culture," Gartner, January 7, 2021, https://www.gartner.com/smarterwithgartner /no-hybrid-workforce-models-wont-dilute-your-culture.

8. Wiles, "Hybrid Workforce Models."

9. Tomi Akitunde, "How Remote Workers Are Creatively Battling Social Isolation," *Work In Progress* (blog), September 30, 2020, https://blog.dropbox .com/topics/work-culture/how-remote-workers-are-creatively-battling-social -isolation.

10. Chris Melore, "Still Working from Home? 7 in 10 Remote Workers Feeling Impact of Social Isolation," StudyFinds, October 13, 2021, https://study finds.org/work-from-home-remote-workers-social-isolation.

11. The Execu|Search Group, "The Great Resignation."

12. Wiles, "Hybrid Workforce Models."

13. Alex Sherman, "Making Sense of Why Executives Are Eager to Get Employees Back in the Office," *CNBC*, March 8, 2022, https://www.cnbc.com/2022 /03/08/return-to-office-why-executives-are-eager-for-workers-to-come-back .html.

14. Herman Milton, "10 Benefits of a Digital Workplace: Why Do Companies Need One?" LumApps, June 14, 2022, https://www.lumapps.com/digital -workplace/digital-workplace-benefits.

15. Avanade, *Global Survey: Companies Are Unprepared for the Arrival of a True Digital Workplace*, 2017, https://www.avanade.com/-/media/asset/research /digital-workplace-global-study.pdf.

16. Irene Hendricks, "Today's Top Talent Expects Inclusion, Flexibility, and Digital Acceleration," Recuiter.com, https://www.recruiter.com/recruiting /todays-top-talent-expects-inclusion-flexibility-and-digital-acceleration.

17. Milton, "10 Benefits of a Digital Workplace."

18. Mearian, "The Great Resignation."

Chapter 3—Security Is Also Changing—
Transforming the Safety of Your Business

1. Gayle Sato, "How Common Is Identity Theft?" *Ask Experian* (blog), January 24, 2021, https://www.experian.com/blogs/ask-experian/how-common-is -identity-theft/.

2. Sato, "How Common Is Identity Theft?"

3. Abi Tyas Tunggal, "What Is the Cost of a Data Breach in 2022?" *UpGuard* (blog), October 3, 2022, https://www.upguard.com/blog/cost-of-data-breach.

4. Tunggal, "What Is the Cost of a Data Breach?"

5. Robert Johnson III, "60 Percent of Small Companies Close within 6 Months of Being Hacked," *Cybercrime Magazine*, January 2, 2019, https://cyber securityventures.com/60-percent-of-small-companies-close-within-6-months -of-being-hacked.

6. Joseph Menn, "U.S. Warns Newly Discovered Malware Could Sabotage Energy Plants," *Washington Post*, April 13, 2022, https://www.washington post.com/technology/2022/04/13/pipedream-malware-russia-lng.

7. Information Systems Security Association, "Cybersecurity Skills Crisis Continues for Fifth Year, Perpetuated by Lack of Business Investment," press release, 2021, https://www.issa.org/cybersecurity-skills-crisis-continues-for -fifth-year-perpetuated-by-lack-of-business-investment/.

8. Information Systems Security Association, "Cybersecurity Skills Crisis Continues."

9. Joe Tidy, "Flaw Prompts 100 Hack Attacks a Minute, Security Company Says," *BBC News*, December 13, 2021, https://www.bbc.com/news /technology-59638308.

10. Tim Hinchliffe, "WEF Global Risks Report Warns of Cyber Pandemic, Erosion of Public Trust & Social Cohesion," *The Sociable* (blog), 2021, https://sociable.co/government-and-policy/wef-global-risks-report-cyber -pandemic-erosion-trust-social-cohesion/.

11. Hinchliffe, "WEF Global Risks Report."

12. Jonathan Camhi, Ragu Gurumurthy, and David Schatsky, "Uncovering the Connection between Digital Maturity and Financial Performance," *Deloitte Insights*, May 26, 2020, https://www2.deloitte.com/content/dam/insights/us /articles/6561_digital-transformation/DI_Digital-transformation.pdf.

13. Camhi, Gurumurthy, and Schatsky, "Uncovering the Connection."

14. Erik Sherman, "94% of the Fortune 1000 Are Seeing Coronavirus Supply Chain Disruptions: Report," *Fortune*, February 21, 2020, https://fortune.com /2020/02/21/fortune-1000-coronavirus-china-supply-chain-impact/.

15. Iryna Bilyk, "Remote Work Culture via Digital Transformation," *Valuer* (blog), April 22, 2021, https://www.valuer.ai/blog/how-digital-transformation -solutions-can-help-you-create-a-remote-work-culture.

16. S. Dixon, "Global Number of Fake Accounts Taken Action on by Facebook from 4th Quarter 2017 to 1st Quarter 2022," Statista, June 2, 2022, https ://www.statista.com/statistics/1013474/facebook-fake-account-removal -quarter.

17. Patrick Hearn, "Digital Identity Is a National Security Issue," War on the Rocks, April 15, 2021, https://warontherocks.com/2021/04/digital-identity -is-a-national-security-issue.

Chapter 4—*Transformation*: The Added Punch of Artificial Intelligence and Machine Learning

1. Mate Labs, "3 Ways AI Can Aid Digital Transformation," *Towards Data Science*, July 15, 2019, https://towardsdatascience.com/3-ways-ai-aids-digital -transformation-4a5965708c45.

2. Joe McKendrick, "AI Adoption Skyrocketed Over the Last 18 Months," *Harvard Business Review*, September 27, 2021, https://hbr.org/2021/09 /ai adoption-skyrocketed-over-the-last-18-months.

3. Gartner, "Gartner Finds 33% of Technology Providers Plan to Invest $1 Million or More in AI Within Two Years," press release, September 29, 2021, https://www.gartner.com/en/newsroom/press-releases/2021-09-29 -gartner-finds-33-percent-of-technology-providers-plan-to-invest-1-million-or -more-in-ai-within-two-years.

4. International Data Corporation, "European Big Data Spending Will Reach $50 Billion This Year, as Companies Focus on Analytics-Enabled Hyper -Automation, Says IDC," press release, September 29, 2021, https://www.idc .com/getdoc.jsp?containerId=prEUR148275921.

5. Gartner, "33% of Technology Providers."

6. B. J. Copeland, "Artificial Intelligence," *Britannica*, updated November 11, 2022, https://www.britannica.com/technology/artificial-intelligence.

7. Sara Brown, "Machine Learning, Explained," MIT Sloan School of Management, April 21, 2021, https://mitsloan.mit.edu/ideas-made-to -matter/machine-learning-explained.

8. Mate Labs, "3 Ways AI Can Aid Digital Transformation."

9. Thomas Baumgartner, Homayoun Hatami, and Maria Valdivieso, "Why Salespeople Need to Develop 'Machine Intelligence,'" *Harvard Business Review*, June 10, 2016, https://hbr.org/2016/06/why-salespeople-need-to -develop-machine-intelligence.

10. Kim del Fierro, "A Digital Transformation Driven by Artificial Intelligence," *Global Trade*, March 28, 2021, https://www.globaltrademag.com/a-digital -transformation-driven-by-artificial-intelligence/.

11. Allen Cone, "Study: AI Faster, More Accurate Than Humans at Analyzing Heart Scans," UPI, March 22, 2018, https://www.upi.com/Health_News /2018/03/22/Study-AI-faster-more-accurate-than-humans-at-analyzing -heart-scans/9451521734122/.

12. Geetika Tandon, "What We've Learned from the Past Decade of Digital Transformation," CMSWire, November 23, 2020, https://www.cmswire.com /information-management/what-weve-learned-from-the-past-decade-of -digital-transformation/.

13. Del Fierro, "A Digital Transformation."

14. Kelly Blum, Matt LoDolce, Gloria Omale, "Gartner Predicts by 2025, 60% of Organizations with Voice of the Customer Programs Will Supplement Traditional Surveys by. Analyzing Voice and Text Interactions with Customers," Gartner, press release, February 21, 2022.

15. "Cybersecurity Remains a Constant Concern for Consumers, Says Study," *Security*, October 23, 2020, https://www.securitymagazine.com/articles /93721-cybersecurity-remains-a-constant-concern-for-consumers-says-study.

16. Louis Columbus, "10 Ways AI and Machine Learning Are Revolutionizing Omnichannel," *Forbes*, February 17, 2019, https://www.forbes.com/sites /louiscolumbus/2019/02/17/10-ways-ai-machine-learning-are-revolutionizing -omnichannel.

Chapter 5—Recognize the Challenges

1. Bob Taylor, "Why 84% of Digital Transformations Are Failing," FROM, https://www.from.digital/is-digital-transformation-worth-it.

2. Peter Bendor-Samuel, "Why Digital Transformations Fail: 3 Exhausting Reasons," Everest Group, August 27, 2019, https://www.everestgrp.com /2019-08-why-digital-transformations-fail-3-exhausting-reasons-blog-51164 .html.

3. Taylor, "84% of Digital Transformations."

4. Jackie Wiles, "Speed Up Your Digital Transformation," Gartner, January 15, 2019, https://www.gartner.com/smarterwithgartner/speed-up-your-digital -business-transformation.

Chapter 6—Leadership Is Everything

1. Elizabeth Mixson, "How to Cultivate Digital Transformation Mindsets," Intelligent Automation Networks, September 9, 2021, https://www .intelligentautomation.network/transformation/articles/how-to-cultivate -digital-transformation-mindsets.

2. Raghav Narsalay, "Driving a Digital Transformation Right Now? Try This," *The Industry X Magazine*, July 16, 2020, https://www.accenture.com/us-en /blogs/industry-digitization/why-collaboration-is-at-the-heart-of-digital -transformation.

3. Narsalay, "Driving a Digital Transformation."

4. Deloitte Insights, *Technology, Media, and Telecommunications Predictions 2022*, 2021, https://www2.deloitte.com/content/dam/insights/articles /GLOB164581_TMT-Predictions-2022/DI_TMT-predictions-2022.pdf.

5. "The 10 Biggest Security Breaches," CardConnect, https://cardconnect.com /launchpointe/payment-security/10-biggest-data-breaches.

6. CardConnect, "The 10 Biggest Security Breaches."

7. Virginia Matthews, "Balancing Ethics and Innovation during Tech Transformation," *Raconteur*, June 18, 2021, https://www.raconteur.net /digital/balancing-ethics-and-innovation-tech-transformation/.

Chapter 7—The Future of Your Organization

1. Deloitte, *Digital CRM 2.0, Building Customer Relationships in the Digital Landscape*, 2019, https://www2.deloitte.com/content/dam/Deloitte/de /Documents/strategy/Deloitte_Digital_Digital_CRM_Study_2.0_2019.pdf.

2. "Digital Customer Experience: Everything to Know in 2022," Qualtrics, 2022, https://www.qualtrics.com/experience-management/customer/what-is -digital-cx/.

3. "Consumers Remind Brands That 'Simplicity' Is the Most Important Part of a Digital Experience," *Netimperative*, June 27, 2018, https://www.net imperative.com/2018/06/27/consumers-remind-brands-that-simplicity-is -the-most-important-part-of-a-digital-experience/.

Chapter 8—Learn

1. Faisal Hoque, V. Sambamurthy, Robert W. Zmud, Tom Trainer, and Carl Wilson, *Winning the 3-Legged Race* (Upper Saddle River: BTM Institute, 2006).

2. Hoque, Sambamurthy, Zmud, Trainer, and Wilson, *Winning the 3-Legged Race*.

3. Hoque, Sambamurthy, Zmud, Trainer, and Wilson, *Winning the 3-Legged Race*.

4. Hoque, Sambamurthy, Zmud, Trainer, and Wilson, *Winning the 3-Legged Race*.

5. Michael Treacey and Fred Wiersema, *The Discipline of Market Leaders: Choose Your Customers, Narrow Your Focus, Dominate Your Market* (New York: Basic Books, 1997).

6. Hoque, Sambamurthy, Zmud, Trainer, and Wilson, *Winning the 3-Legged Race*.

7. Hoque, Sambamurthy, Zmud, Trainer, and Wilson, *Winning the 3-Legged Race*.

8. Hoque, Sambamurthy, Zmud, Trainer, and Wilson, *Winning the 3-Legged Race*.

9. Hoque, Sambamurthy, Zmud, Trainer, and Wilson, *Winning the 3-Legged Race*.

10. Eric Kimberg, "Top 10 Digital Transformation Failures of All Time, Selected by an ERP Expert Witness," Third Stage Consulting Group, April 8, 2021, https://www.thirdstage-consulting.com/top-10-digital-transformation -failures-of-all-time-selected-by-an-erp-expert-witness/.

11. Ethan Bernstein, Joost Minnaar, and Michael Y. Lee, "How Companies Are Using Tech to Give Employees More Autonomy," *Harvard Business Review*, January 28, 2022, https://hbr.org/2022/01/how-companies-are-using-tech -to-give-employees-more-autonomy.

12. Scott King, "Digital Transformation Successes and Failures," Krista, https ://kristasoft.com/digital-transformation-success/.

Chapter 9—Investigate

1. Faisal Hoque, V. Sambamurthy, Robert W. Zmud, Tom Trainer, and Carl Wilson, *Winning the 3-Legged Race* (Upper Saddle River: BTM Institute, 2006).

2. Hoque, Sambamurthy, Zmud, Trainer, and Wilson, *Winning the 3-Legged Race*.

3. Hoque, Sambamurthy, Zmud, Trainer, and Wilson, *Winning the 3-Legged Race*.

4. "PEST analysis," Wikipedia, last updated November 5, 2022, https://en .wikipedia.org/wiki/PEST_analysis.

5. Hoque, Sambamurthy, Zmud, Trainer, and Wilson, *Winning the 3-Legged Race*.

6. Hoque, Sambamurthy, Zmud, Trainer, and Wilson, *Winning the 3-Legged Race*.

7. M. E. Porter, "How Competitive Forces Shape Strategy," *Harvard Business Review*, March/April 1979, https://hbr.org/2008/01/the-five-competitive -forces-that-shape-strategy.

8. Hoque, Sambamurthy, Zmud, Trainer, and Wilson, *Winning the 3-Legged Race*.

Chapter 10—Formulate

1. Faisal Hoque, V. Sambamurthy, Robert W. Zmud, Tom Trainer, and Carl Wilson, *Winning the 3-Legged Race* (Upper Saddle River: BTM Institute, 2006).

2. Hoque, Sambamurthy, Zmud, Trainer, and Wilson, *Winning the 3-Legged Race*.

Chapter 11—Take Off

1. Faisal Hoque, V. Sambamurthy, Robert W. Zmud, Tom Trainer, and Carl Wilson, *Winning the 3-Legged Race* (Upper Saddle River: BTM Institute, 2006).

Chapter 12—Study

1. Jaak Jurison, "Productivity," in *Encyclopedia of Information Systems*, ed. Hossein Bidgoli (Elsevier, 2003), 517–28.

2. Daniel L. Goelzer, "The Costs & Benefits of Sarbanes-Oxley Section 404," Public Company Accounting Oversight Board, March 21, 2005, https ://pcaobus.org/news-events/speeches/speech-detail/the-costs-benefits-of-sarbanes-oxley-section-404_126.

3. Hoque, Sambamurthy, Zmud, Trainer, and Wilson, *Winning the 3-Legged Race*.

4. Hoque, Sambamurthy, Zmud, Trainer, and Wilson, *Winning the 3-Legged Race*.

5. Faisal Hoque, V. Sambamurthy, Robert W. Zmud, Tom Trainer, and Carl Wilson, *Winning the 3-Legged Race* (Upper Saddle River: BTM Institute, 2006).

6. Hoque, Sambamurthy, Zmud, Trainer, and Wilson, *Winning the 3-Legged Race*.